William Pitt

Speech of the Right Honourable William Pitt

In the House of Commons, Thursday, January 31, 1799

William Pitt

Speech of the Right Honourable William Pitt
In the House of Commons, Thursday, January 31, 1799

ISBN/EAN: 9783337186128

Printed in Europe, USA, Canada, Australia, Japan

Cover: Foto ©Suzi / pixelio.de

More available books at **www.hansebooks.com**

SPEECH

OF THE

RIGHT HONOURABLE

WILLIAM PITT,

IN THE

HOUSE OF COMMONS,

THURSDAY, JANUARY 31, 1799,

On offering to the House the RESOLUTIONS which he proposed as the BASIS OF AN UNION between GREAT BRITAIN AND IRELAND,

To which are added the SPEECHES of the Right Honourable JOHN FOSTER, on the 12th and 15th of *August*, 1785, on the BILL *for effectuating the* INTERCOURSE *and* COMMERCE *between* Great Britain *and* Ireland, *on permanent and equitable Principles, for the mutual Benefit of both Kingdoms.*

DUBLIN:

PRINTED BY JOHN EXSHAW. 08, GRAFTON-STREET.

1799.

SPEECH

OF THE

Right Hon. William Pitt,

&c. &c.

The Speaker having read His Majesty's
Message, *viz.*

GEORGE REX.

" His Majesty is perfuaded that the unremitting induſtry
" with which our enemies perſevere in their avowed de-
" ſign of effecting the Separation of Ireland from this
" Kingdom, cannot fail to engage the particular attention
" of Parliament; and His Majeſty recommends it to this
" Houſe to conſider of the moſt effectual means of counter-
" acting and finally defeating this deſign; and he truſts
" that a review of all the circumſtances which have
" recently occurred (joined to the ſentiment of mutual
" affection and common intereſt,) will diſpoſe the Parlia-
" ment of both Kingdoms to provide, in the manner
" which

" which they shall judge most expedient, for settling such
" a complete and final adjustment as may best tend to im-
" prove and perpetuate a Connection essential for their
" common security, and to augment and consolidate the
" Strength, Power, and Resources of the British Empire."

G. R.

Mr. PITT *rose, and spoke as follows*:

SIR,

WHEN I proposed to the House, the last time this subject was before them, to fix this day for the further consideration of His Majesty's Message, I certainly indulged the hope that the result of a similar communication to the Parliament of Ireland would have opened a more favourable Prospect than at present exists, of the speedy accomplishment of a measure which I then stated, and which I still consider, to be of the greatest importance to the power, the stability, and the general welfare of the Empire; to the immediate interests of both kingdoms—and more particularly to the peace, the tranquillity, and the safety of Ireland: in this hope, I am sorry to say, I have for the present been disappointed, by the proceedings of the Irish House of Commons, of
which

which we have been informed since this subject was last under consideration.

I feel and know that the Parliament of Ireland possesses the power, the intire competence, on the behalf of that country, alike to accept or reject a proposition of this nature—a power which I am by no means inclined to dispute. I see that at the present moment one House of Parliament in Ireland has expressed a repugnance, even to the consideration of this measure.——Feeling, Sir, as I have already stated, that it is important, not only as it tends to the general prosperity of the Empire of Great Britain, but (what, under every situation, must always be to me an object of the greatest moment) feeling that it was designed and calculated to increase the prosperity and ensure the safety of Ireland, I must have seen with the deepest regret that, at the very first moment, and before the nature of the measure could be known, it was so received.

But whatever may have been my feelings upon this subject, knowing that it is the undoubted right of the Legiflature of Ireland to reject or to adopt fuch meafures as may appear to them injurious or beneficial, far be it from me to fpeak of its determination in any other terms but thofe of refpect. Let it not, therefore, be imagined that I am inclined to prefs any fentiment, however calculated it may appear to me to benefit every member of the Empire, in any manner which may lead to hoftile difcuffion between two kingdoms, whofe mutual happinefs and fafety depend upon their being ftrictly and cordially united. But while I admit and refpect the rights of the Parliament of Ireland, I feel that, as a Member of the Parliament of Great Britain, I alfo have a Right to exercife, and a Duty to perform. That Duty is to exprefs, as diftinctly as I can, the general nature and outline of the Plan, which, in my confcience, I think would tend in the ftrongeft manner to enfure the fafety and the happinefs of both kingdoms.

While I feel, therefore, that as long as the Houfe of Commons of Ireland view the fubject in the light they do at prefent, there is no chance
of

of its adoption, I do not think that I ought on that account to abstain from submitting it to the consideration of this Parliament; on the contrary I think it only the more necessary to explain distinctly the principles of the Measure, and to state the grounds upon which it appears to me to be entitled to the approbation of the Legislature.

If Parliament, when it is in possession of the basis upon which this Plan is founded, and of its general outline, should be of opinion with me, that it is founded upon fair, just, and equitable principles, calculated to produce mutual advantages to the two Kingdoms—if Parliament, I say, upon full explanation, and after mature deliberation, should be of that opinion, I should propose that its determination should remain recorded as that by which the Parliament of Great Britain were ready to abide, leaving it to the Legislature of Ireland to reject or to adopt hereafter, upon a full consideration of the subject.

There is no man will deny that in a great question of this nature, involving in it objects which,

which, in the firſt inſtance, are more likely to be decided upon by paſſion than by judgment; in a queſtion in which an honeſt but, I muſt be allowed to ſay, a miſtaken ſenſe of National Pride is ſo likely to operate, that much miſconſtruction and miſconception muſt inevitably happen. It therefore becomes the more neceſſary that the intentions of the Government which propoſes the Meaſure, and the principles of the Meaſure itſelf, ſhould be diſtinctly underſtood. But, Sir, in ſtating that intention and thoſe principles, I look to ſomething more than a mere vindication of Government for having propoſed the Meaſure. I do entertain a confidence, even under the apparent diſcouragement of the opinion expreſſed by the Iriſh Houſe of Commons, that this Meaſure is founded upon ſuch clear, ſuch demonſtrable grounds of utility, is ſo calculated to add to the ſtrength and power of the Empire, (in which the ſafety of Ireland is included, and from which it never can be ſeparated) and is attended with ſo many advantages to Ireland in particular, that all that can be neceſſary for its ultimate adoption is, that it ſhould be ſtated diſtinctly, temperately, and fully, and that it ſhould be left to unprejudiced,

diced, the difpaffionate, the fober judgment of the Parliament of Ireland. I wifh that thofe whofe interefts are involved in this meafure fhould have time for its confideration—I wifh that time fhould be given to the Landed, to the Mercantile and Manufacturing Intereft, that they fhould look at it with all its bearings, and that they fhould cooly examine and fift the popular arguments by which it has been oppofed, and that then they fhould give their deliberate and final judgment.

I am the more encouraged in this hope of the ultimate fuccefs of this meafure, when I fee, notwithftanding all the prejudices which it has excited, that barely more than one-half of the members that attended the Houfe of Commons were adverfe to it; and that in the other Houfe of Parliament in Ireland, containing, as it does, fo large a portion of the property of the kingdom, it was approved of by a large majority.—When I have reafon to believe that the fentiments of a large part of the People of that Country are favourable to it; and that much of the Manufacturing, and of the Commercial Intereft of Ireland are already fenfible

how

how much it is calculated to promote their advantage, I think, when it is more deliberately examined, and when it is seen in what temper it is here proposed and discussed, that it will still terminate in that which can alone be a fortunate result.

It would be vain indeed to hope that a proposition upon which prejudices are so likely to operate, and which is so liable to misconception, should be unanimously approved. But the approbation I hope for is, that of the Parliament of Ireland, and of the intelligent part of the Public of that Country. It is with a view to this object that I think it my duty to bring this measure forward at present; not for the sake of urging its immediate adoption, but that it may be known and recorded; that the intention of the British Parliament may be known, in the hope that it will produce similar sentiments among our Countrymen in Ireland. With this view it is my intention not to go at present into any detailed statement of the plan, because should it ultimately be adopted, the minuter parts must necessarily become the objects of much distinct discussion; but to give such a general statement of the nature of

the

the meafure as will enable the Houfe to form a correct judgment upon it.

I fhall therefore, Sir, before I fit down, open to the Houfe a ftring of Refolutions, comprifing the general heads of this plan. It will be neceffary for me, for the purpofe of difcuffing thofe Refolutions with regularity and convenience, to move that the Houfe fhould refolve itfelf into a Committee. And I have already ftated, that it is not my intention then to prefs the Committee to come to an immediate decifion upon the Refolutions; but if, upon full and deliberate examination, the Refolutions which I fhall have the honour to propofe, and which contain as much as is neceffary for an outline of the plan, fhall be approved, my opinion is, that nothing can contribute more to obviate any doubts and diffatisfaction which may exift, than that Parliament fhould adopt thofe Refolutions, and that it fhould then humbly leave them at the foot of the Throne, leaving it to His Majesty's wifdom to communicate them to the Parliament of Ireland, whenever circumftances fhould appear favourable to fuch a Meafure. I fhall therefore, Sir, proceed as fhortly shortly as I can to state to the House the nature of the Resolutions, and of the Address which I shall propose to accompany them, if it should be the pleasure of the House to adopt them.

Having now, Sir, explained to the House the mode I mean to pursue, and my reasons for persisting, under the present circumstances, in submitting this Measure to the consideration of Parliament, I will endeavour to state the general grounds on which it rests, the general arguments by which it is recommended, and to give a short view of the particulars of the Plan.

As to the general principle upon which the whole of this Measure is founded, I am happy to observe, from what passed upon a former occasion, that there is not a probability of any difference of opinion. The general principle, to which both sides of the House perfectly acceded, is, that a perpetual Connection between Great Britain and Ireland was essential to the interests of both. The only Honourable Gentleman who, when this subject was before the House on a

former

former day, oppofed the confideration of the Plan altogether, ftated, in terms as ftrong as I could wifh, the neceffity of preferving the ftricteft Connection between the two Countries. I moft cordially agree with him in that opinion, but I then ftated, that I do not barely wifh for the maintenance of that Connection as tending to add to the general ftrength of the Empire, but I wifh for the maintenance of it with a peculiar regard to the local interefts of Ireland, with a regard to every thing that can give to Ireland its due weight and importance, as a great member of the Empire. I wifh for it with a view of giving to that Country the means of improving all its great natural Refources, and of giving it a full participation of all thofe bleffings which this Country fo eminently enjoys.

Confidering the fubject in this point of view, and affuming it as a propofition not to be controverted, that it is the duty of thofe who wifh to promote the Intereft and Profperity of both Countries, to maintain the ftrongeft connection between them, let me afk, what is the fituation of Affairs that has called us to the difcuffion of this fubject?

subject? This very connection, the necessity of which has been admitted on all hands, has been attacked by Foreign Enemies, and by Domestic Traitors. The dissolution of that connection is the great object of the hostility of the common Enemies of both Countries, it is almost the only remaining hope with which they now continue the contest. Baffled and defeated as they have hitherto been, they still retain the hope, they are still meditating attempts, to dissolve that connection. God grant that in this instance the same favour of Divine Providence, which has in so many instances protected this Empire, may again interpose in our favour, and that the attempts of the Enemy to separate the two Countries, may tend ultimately to knit them more closely together, to strengthen a Connection, the best pledge for the happiness of both, and so add to that power which forms the chief barrier to the civilized world, against the destructive principles, the dangerous projects, and the unexampled usurpation of France. This Connection has been attacked not only by the avowed Enemies of both Countries, but by internal Treason, acting in concert with the designs of the Enemy. Internal Treason,

Treason, which ingrafted Jacobinism on those diseases which necessarily grew out of the State and Condition of Ireland.

Thinking, then, as we all must think, that a close Connection with Ireland is essential to the interests of both Countries, and seeing how much this Connection is attacked, let it not be insinuated that it is unnecessary, much less improper, at this arduous and important crisis, to see whether some new arrangements, some fundamental regulations, are not necessary, to guard against the threatened danger. The foreign and domestic Enemies of these kingdoms have shewn, that they think this the vulnerable point in which they may be most succesfully attacked; let us derive advantage, if we can, from the hostility of our Enemies — let us profit by the designs of an Enemy, who, if his conduct displays no true wisdom, at least possesses in an eminent degree that species of wisdom which is calculated for the promotion of mischief. They know upon what footing that Connection rests at this moment between the two Countries, and they feel the most ardent hope, that the two Parliaments will be infatuated

enough

enough not to render their designs abortive, by fixing that Connection upon a more solid basis.

These circumstances I am sure will not be denied. And if upon other grounds we had any doubt, these circumstances alone ought to induce us, deliberately and dispassionately, to review the situation of the two Countries, and to endeavour to find out a proper remedy for an evil, the existence of which is but too apparent. It requires but a moment's reflection, for any man who has marked the progress of events, to decide upon the true state and character of this Connection. It is evidently one which does not afford that security which, even in times less dangerous and less critical than the present, would have been necessary, to enable the empire to avail itself of its strength and its resources.

When I last addressed the House on this subject, I stated that the settlement, which was made in 1782, so far from deserving the name of a Final Adjustment, was one that left the Connection between Great Britain and Ireland exposed to all the attacks of Party, and all the effects of accident.

accident. That Settlement consisted in the demolition of the System which before held the two Countries together. Let me not be understood as expressing any regret at the termination of that System. I disapproved of it, because I thought it was one unworthy the liberality of Great Britain, and injurious to the interests of Ireland. But to call that a System in itself—to call that a glorious fabric of human wisdom—which is no more than the mere demolition of another System—is a perversion of terms which, however prevalent of late, can only be the effect of gross misconception, or of great hypocrisy. We boast that we have done every thing, when we have merely destroyed all that before existed, without substituting any thing in its place. Such was the *Final Adjustment* of 1782; and I can prove it to be so, not only from the plainest reasoning, but I can prove it by the opinion expressed by the British Parliament at that very time. I can prove it by the opinion expressed by those very Ministers by whom it was proposed and conducted. I can prove it by the opinion of that very Government who boast of having effected a Final Adjustment. I refer, for what I have said, to proofs which they will find it

very

very difficult to answer; I mean their own acts, which will plainly shew that they were of opinion that a new System would be necessary. But, Sir, I will go farther—I will also produce the authority of one of those whose influence, on the present occasion, has been peculiarly exerted to prevent the discussion of the question in Ireland—of one, of whom I do not wish to speak but with respect, but for whom, nevertheless, I should convey an idea of more respect, than I can now feel to be due to him, if I were merely to describe him as the person who fills the same situation, in the House of Commons of Ireland, which you, Sir, hold among us, and of which on all occasions *you* discharge the duties with a dignity and impartiality which reflects so much credit on yourself, and so well supports the character and authority of the House.

On a former night, I read an Extract from the Journals, to shew what was the opinion even of those by whom the Final Adjustment was proposed, of that Measure. It would there appear, that the Message was sent to the Parliament of Ireland, recommending to them the adoption of

some

some Plan for a Final Adjustment between the two Countries, and wishing to know what were the grounds of the grievances of which they complained. In answer to this Message, the Parliament of Ireland stated certain grievances, the principal of which was, the power claimed by the Parliament of Great Britain of making Laws to bind Ireland; but, with respect to that part of the Message which related to the propriety of adopting some Measures for a final adjustment between the two Countries, they were wholly silent. This Address was laid before the Parliament of Great Britain, to whom a similar Message had been sent, and on that ground was moved the Repeal of what was called the Declaratory Act, which Motion was assented to by the British Parliament. This satisfaction was complete to Ireland, as far as related to the grievance of which her Parliament had complained, viz. the Power of the British Parliament of making Laws for Ireland, because, by the Repeal of the Declaratory Act, that power was given up. But so far was the Minister of that day from considering that the Repeal of that Law finally terminated all differences, and established the Connection between the two Coun-

D tries

tries upon a folid bafis, that he thought it neceffary to move that a farther Settlement was indif-
penfable for the maintenance of that Connection.

[Mr. SHERIDAN acrofs the Table, defired that that part of the Journals to which Mr. PITT alluded, might be read.]

Mr. PITT continued. Sir, I have ftated the fubftance of the Journals correctly; they were read on a former night, and the Honourable Gentleman may, if he choofes, have them read again.* If he does he will find that they fully juftify the ftatement I have made, but I beg that at prefent I may not be interrupted. I do maintain, that upon a reference to the Journals of the period to which I have alluded, it will appear that a farther agreement between Great Britain and Ireland is there ftated, in the opinion of the Adminiftration of the day, to be abfolutely neceffary.

I beg farther to ftate, that after the Bill of which fo much has been faid, was paffed, an Addrefs to HIS MAJESTY was moved and carried, praying him to take fuch further meafures as to him feemed proper, to ftrengthen the Connection

* Vide Appendix.

between

between the two Countries. His Majesty's most Gracious Anſwer, ſtating, that in compliance with the Addreſs, he would immediately take ſuch meaſures as might be neceſſary for that purpoſe, was delivered to the Houſe by an Honourable Gentleman who then filled the office of Secretary of State, and whom we have not lately ſeen in the Houſe, though he ſtill continues to be a Member of it. I do aſſert, without the leaſt fear of contradiction from any Gentleman whatever, that it was in the contemplation of the Government of that day, to adopt ſome meaſures of the nature alluded to in the Addreſs; ſince that period, however, no ſuch meaſure has been taken. I do alſo maintain, that that very ſyſtem which by theſe very Miniſters who brought it forward was found to be imperfect, even for the purpoſe of maintaining the Connection between the two Countries, remains at this moment in the ſame imperfect ſtate. It leaves the two Countries with ſeparate and independent Legiſlatures, connected only with this tie, that the Third Eſtate in both Countries is the ſame—that the Executive Government is the ſame—that the Crown exerciſes its power of aſſenting to Iriſh Acts of Parliament under the Great Seal of Great Britain, and by the advice of British Ministers.

This is the only principle of Connection which is left by the Final Adjustment of 1782. Whether this is a sufficient tie to unite them in time of Peace; whether in time of War it is sufficient to consolidate their strength against a Common Enemy; whether it is sufficient to guard against those local jealousies which must necessarily sometimes exist between countries so connected; whether it is calculated to give to Ireland all the important commercial and political advantages which she would derive from a closer Connection with Great Britain; whether it can give to both Nations that degree of strength and prosperity which must be the result of such a Measure as the present, I believe need only to be stated to be decided.

But I have already said, that I have upon this point, the authority of an opinion to which I before alluded—an opinion delivered upon a very important Measure, very soon after the Final Adjustment of 1782. The Measure to which I refer, was that of the Commercial Propositions which
were

were brought forward in 1785. I am not now going to enter into a difcuffion of the merits of that Meafure. The beft, perhaps, that can be faid of it is, that it went as far as circumftances would then permit, to draw the two Countries to a clofer Connection. But thofe who think that the Adjuftment of 1782 was final, and that it contained all that was neceffary for the eftablifhment of the Connection between the two Countries upon a firm bafis, can hardly contend that the Commercial Propofitions of 1785 were neceffary to prevent the danger of feparation between the two Countries, and to prevent the conflicting operation of Independent Legiflatures. Yet, if I am not miftaken, there will be found, upon a reference to better Records than thofe in which Parliamentary Debates are ufually ftated (I mean a ftatement of what paffed in the difcuffion upon thofe Propofitions fourteen years ago, made, as I have underftood, by fome of the principal parties themfelves) that the CHANCELLOR of the EXCHEQUER of that day in Ireland, in a Debate upon the Irifh Propofitions, held this language—" If " this infatuated Couutry gives up the prefent of- " fer, fhe may look for it again in vain." Here the

* Right

Right Honourable Gentleman was happily mistaken; Ireland has again had the offer of the fame advantages, but more complete, and in all refpects better calculated to attain their object; and this offer the Right Honourable Gentleman has exerted all his influence to reject. But he goes on to fay—" THINGS CANNOT REMAIN AS
" THEY ARE—Commercial jealoufy is roufed—
" it will encreafe with *two independent Legiflatures*
" —and without an united intereft in commerce,
" in a commercial Empire, political Union will
" receive many fhocks, and *feparation of intereft*
" muft threaten *feparation of Connection,* which
" every *honeft Irifhman* muft fhudder to look at,
" as a poffible event."

Gentlemen will have the goodnefs to obferve, that I am not now quoting thefe expreffions as pledges given by that Right Honourable Gentleman that he would fupport a propofal for a Union between the two Countries, but I am adducing them to prove that the fituation of the two Countries after the Final Adjuftment of 1782, was fuch, in his opinion, as led to the danger of a feparation between them. I am not now arguing

that

that a Legiflative Union is the only meafure which can poffibly be adopted, but I am contending that the Adjuftment of 1782 was never confidered as final, by thofe who now ftate it to be fo as an argument againft the confideration of the prefent meafure. How the Honourable Gentleman on the other fide of the Houfe will evade this authority I do not know ;—an authority too, which, I muft obferve, he feems much more inclined to treat with refpect than he was formerly.

But, Sir, it does not ftop there. What is the evil to which he alludes? Commercial jealoufies between two Countries acting upon the laws of two independent Legiflatures, and from the danger of thofe Legiflatures acting with jealoufy to each other.—How can this evil be remedied? By two means only; either by fome Compact entered into by the Legiflatures of the two Countries refpecting the mode of forming their commercial regulations, or elfe by blending the two Legiflatures together; thefe are the only two means. I defy the wit of man to point out a third. The mode of compact was propofed in 1785, but unfortunately, in fpite of that Right Honourable

Gentleman's

Gentleman's eloquence and authority, who then stated the importance of guarding against the evil, it so happened that doctrines, derived chiefly from this side of the water, succeeded in convincing the Parliament of Ireland, that it would be inconsistent with their independence, to enter into any compact whatever. We have then the authority of that Rt. Honourable Gentleman to whom I have so often alluded, that the unsettled state in which the matter was left, would give, "Political Union many shocks, and lead to a separation of Connection." The experiment of a mutual Compact has been tried without success; the arrangement of that sort, which was proposed in 1785, in order to obviate the inconveniences stated by the Right Honourable Gentleman, was then attacked with the same success against his authority, as another and more effectual remedy has recently experienced under his auspices. The result then is, you must remain in the state which that Right Honourable Gentleman has described, with the seeds of separation in the system now established, and with the Connection, on which the mutual prosperity of both Countries depends in danger of being hourly dissolved, or you must again
recur

recur to the proposal of a compact similar to that rejected in 1785, or you must resort to the best and most effectual remedy,——A LEGISLATIVE UNION.

I have dwelt longer, perhaps, upon this part of the subject than was absolutely necessary, because I believe there is scarcely any man who has ever asked himself, whether there is a solid, permanent system of Connection between the two Countries, who could, upon reflection, answer the question in the affirmative. But besides the authorities of the persons who made the arrangement in 1782, and of those who have since treated of it, to shew that it was not deemed to be final and complete; I have further the test of experience to shew how imperfect it was, and how inadequate in practice to the great object of cementing the Connection, and placing it beyond the danger of being dissolved. In the single instance, which has occurred (and that a melancholy one which all of us deplored) in which we could feel the effects of two jarring Legislatures we did feel it. On that occasion, it might have produced the most signal calamities, had we not been

been rescued from its danger by an event, to which no man can now look back without feeling the utmost joy and exultation; feelings, which subsequent circumstances have served to heighten and confirm. Every Gentleman will know, that I must allude to the Regency. With two independent Legislatures, acting upon different principles, it was accident alone that preserved the identity of the Executive Power, which is the bond and security of the Connection: And even then the Executive authority, though vested in one person, would have been held by him by two different tenures, by one tenure in England, by another in Ireland, had not the interposition of Providence prevented a circumstance pregnant with the most imminent perils, and which might have operated to a separation of the two kingdoms.

After seeing the recorded opinion of Parliament, of those who made the arrangement of 1782, and after the decided testimony of experience on the subject, within the short period of fixteen years, perhaps, it is hardly necessary to appeal to farther proofs

proofs of its inadequacy, or to defire Gentlemen to look forward to poffible cafes, which I could eafily put, and which will naturally fuggeft themfelves to the minds of all, who chufe to turn their attention to the fubject.

But when we confider the diftinct powers poffeffed by the two Legiflatures on all the great queftions of Peace and War, of alliances and confederacies,—(for they each have in principle, a right to difcufs them and decide upon them, though one of them has hitherto been wifely reftrained by difcretion, from the exercife of that right),—have we not feen circumftances to induce us to think it poffible, at leaft, that on fome of thefe important queftions the opinions and decifions of the two Parliaments might have been at variance? Are we talking of an indiffoluble Connection, when we fee it thus perpetually liable to be endangered? Can we really think that the interefts of the Empire, or of its different branches reft upon a fafe and folid bafis at prefent? I am anxious to difcufs this point clofely with any man, either here or in Ireland. Will it it be said, that the Parliament of the latter Country is bound by our decision on the question of Peace or War? And if not so bound, will any man, looking at human Nature as it is, contend, that there is a sufficient certainty that the decision on that important subject will always be the same in both countries? I should be glad to receive a distinct answer to this question, from the Honourable Gentleman who has declared himself to be as warm a friend to the Connection between the two Countries as I am.

Suppose, for instance, that the present war, which the Parliament of Great Britain considers to be just and necessary, had been voted by the Irish Parliament, to be unjust, unnecessary, extravagant, and hostile to the principles of humanity and freedom.—Would that Parliament have been bound by this Country? If not;—what security have we, at a moment the most important to our common interest and common salvation, that the two Kingdoms should have but one friend and foe? I repeat it; I am eager to hear what can be said in justification of a basis so imperfect and unfound,

found, and liable to be shaken by so many accidents. I have already observed, that in the peculiar circumstances of the present moment, we may find strong reasons to prove the necessity of correcting the system of Connection between this Country and Ireland, of supplying its imperfections, and strengthening its weakness, than are to be found at any former period.

Having thus stated, and I think sufficiently proved, that the Settlement of 1782, in every point of view in which it can be considered, is imperfect, and inadequate to the object of maintaining the connection between the two kingdoms, I proceed next to the circumstances which peculiarly call upon us at the present moment to remedy that imperfection.

This Country is at this time engaged in the most important, and momentous conflict that ever occurred in the History of the World; a conflict in which Great Britain is distinguished for having made the only manly and successful stand against the common enemies of civilized society. We see the point in which that Enemy think us the

most

most assailable—Are we not then bound in policy and prudence, to strengthen that vulnerable point, involved as we are in a contest of Liberty against Despotism—of Property against Plunder and Rapine—of Religion and Order against Impiety and Anarchy? There was a time when this would have been termed declamation; but, unfortunately, long and bitter experience has taught us to feel that it is only the feeble and imperfect representation of those calamities (the result of French Principles and French Arms) which are attested by the wounds of a bleeding world.

Is there a man who does not admit the importance of a measure which, at such a crisis, may augment the strength of the Empire, and thereby ensure its safety? Would not that benefit to Ireland be of itself so solid, so inestimable, that, in comparison with it, all Commercial Interests, and the preservation of local habits and manners, would be trifling, even if they were endangered by the present measure;—which they undoubtedly are not? The people of Ireland are proud, I believe, of being associated with us in the great contest in which we are engaged, and must feel

the

the advantage of augmenting the general force of the Empire. That the prefent meafure is calculated to produce that effect, is a propofition which I think cannot be difputed. There is not in any Court of Europe a Statefman fo ill informed as not to know, that the general power of the Empire would be increafed to a very great extent indeed, by fuch a confolidation of the ftrength of the two kingdoms. In the courfe of the Century every writer of any information on the fubject has held the fame language, and in the general ftrength of the Empire both Kingdoms are more concerned than in any particular interefts which may belong to either. If we were to afk the Minifters of our Allies, what meafure they thought the moft likely to augment the power of the Britifh Empire, and confequently increafe that ftrength by which they were now protected—if we were to afk the Agent of our Enemies, what meafure would be the moft likely to render their defigns abortive—the anfwer would be the fame in both cafes, viz. the firm confolidation of every part of the Empire.

There is another confideration well worth attention. Recollect what are the peculiar means by which we have been enabled to refift the unequalled and eccentric efforts of France, without any diminution, nay, with an increafe, of our general profperity—what, but the great Commercial Refources which we poffefs? A Meafure, then, which muft communicate to fuch a mighty Limb of the Empire as Ireland, all the Commercial advantages which Great Britain poffeffes, which will open the markets of the one Country to the other, which will give them both the common ufe of their Capital, muft, by diffufing a large portion of wealth into Ireland, confiderably increafe the Refources, and confequently the ftrength, of the whole Empire.

But it is not merely in this general view, that I think the Queftion ought to be confidered.—We ought to look to it with a view peculiarly to the permanent Intereft and fecurity of Ireland. When that Country was threatened with the double danger of hoftile attacks by Enemies without, and of Treafon within, from what quarter did fhe

derive

derive the means of her deliverance?—from the Naval Force of Great Britain—from the voluntary exertions of her Military of every defcription, not called for by Law—and from her pecuniary refources, added to the loyalty and energy of the Inhabitants of Ireland itfelf;—of which it is impoffible to fpeak with too much praife, and which fhews how well they deferve to be called the Brethren of Britons. Their own courage might, perhaps have ultimately fucceeded, in repelling the dangers by which they were threatened, but it would have been after a long conteft, and after having waded through feas of blood. Are we fure that the fame ready and effectual affiftance which we have happily afforded, on the prefent occafion, will be always equally within our power? Great Britain has always felt a common intereft in the fafety of Ireland; but that common intereft was never fo obvious and urgent as when the Common Enemy made her attack upon Great Britain, through the medium of Ireland, and when their attack upon Ireland went to deprive her of her Connection with Great Britain, and to fubftitute in ftead, the new Government of the French Republic. When that danger threatened Ireland, the purſe of Great Britain was open for the wants of Ireland, as for the neceſſities of England.

I do not, Sir, ſtate theſe circumſtances, as upbraiding Ireland for the benefits we have conferred; far from it; but I ſtate them with pleaſure, as ſhewing the friendſhip and good will with which this Country has acted towards her. But if ſtruggles of this ſort may and muſt return again, if the worſt dangers are thoſe which are yet to come, dangers which may be greater from being more diſguiſed—if thoſe ſituations may ariſe when the ſame means of relief are not in our power, what is the remedy that reaſon and policy point out? It is to identify them with us—it is to make them part of the ſame Community, by giving them a full ſhare of thoſe accumulated bleſſings which are diffuſed throughout Great Britain; it is, in a word, by giving them a full participation of the Wealth, the Powers and the Glory of the Britiſh Empire. If then this Meaſure comes recommended not only by the obvious defects of the ſyſtem which now exiſts, but that it has alſo the pre-eminent recommendation of increaſing the general power of the Empire, and of guarding

againſt

against future danger from the Common Enemy, we are next to confider it as to its effects upon the internal condition of Ireland.

I know perfectly well, that as long as Ireland is feparated from Great Britain, any attempt on our part to provide meafures which we might think falutary, as refpecting queftions of contending fects or parties, of the claimed rights of the Catholics, or of the precautions neceffary for the fecurity of the Proteftants—I know that all thefe, though they may have been brought forward by the very perfons who are the advocates of the Final Adjuftment in 1782, were, in fact, attacks upon the Independence of the Irifh Parliament, and attempts to ufurp the Right of deciding on points which can only be brought within our province by compact. Until the Kingdoms are united, any attempt to make regulations here for the internal ftate of Ireland muft certainly be a violation of her Independence. But feeling as I do, for their interefts and their welfare, I cannot be inattentive to the events that are paffing before me; I muft therefore repeat, that whoever looks at the circumftances to which I have alluded—whoever confiders that the Enemy

have

have shewn by their conduct, that they considered Ireland as the weakest and most vulnerable part of the Empire; whoever reflects upon those dreadful and inexcusable cruelties instigated by the Enemies of both Countries, and upon those lamentable severities by which the exertions for the defence of Ireland were unhappily, but unavoidably, attended, and the necessity of which is itself one great aggravation of the Crimes and Treasons which led to them, must feel that, as it now stands composed, in the hostile division of its Sects, in the animosities existing between ancient Settlers and original Inhabitants, in the ignorance and want of Civilization, which marks that Country more than almost any other Country in Europe, in the unfortunate prevalence of Jacobin Principles, arising from these causes, and augmenting their malignity, and which have produced that distressed state which we now deplore; every one, I say, who reflects upon all these circumstances, must agree with me in thinking, that there is no cure but in the formation of a General Imperial Legislature, free alike from terror and from resentment, removed from the danger and agitation, and uninflamed by the prejudices and passions of that distracted Country.

I know

I know that it is impoffible, if we wifh to confider this fubject properly, to confider it in any other point of view than as it affects the Empire in general. I know that the interefts of the two Countries muft be taken together, and that a man cannot fpeak as a true Englifhman, unlefs he fpeaks as a true Irifhman, nor as a true Irifhman, unlefs he fpeaks as a true Englifhman: But if it was poffible to feparate them, and I could confider myfelf as addreffing you, not as interefted for the Empire at large, but for Ireland alone, I fhould fay, that it would be indifpenfably neceffary, for the fake of that Country, to compofe its prefent diftractions, by the adoption of another fyftem:—I fhould fay, that the eftablifhment of an Imperial Legiflature was the only means of healing its wounds and of reftoring it to tranquillity. I muft here take the liberty of alluding to fome topics which were touched upon during the difcuffion of the former night.

Among the great and known defects of Ireland, one of the moft prominent features is, its want of induftry and a capital; how are thofe wants to be fupplied, but by blending more clofely with Ireland,

Ireland, the induſtry and the capital of this Country. But, above all, in the great leading diſtinctions between the People of Ireland, I mean their religious diſtinctions, what is their ſituation?— The Proteſtant feels that the claims of the Catholics threaten the exiſtence of the Proteſtant aſcendancy; while, on the other hand, the great body of Catholics feel the eſtabliſhment of the National Church, and their excluſion from the exerciſe of certain rights and privileges, a grievance. Between the two, it becomes a matter of difficulty in the minds of many perſons, whether it would be better to liſten only to the fears of the former, or to grant the claims of the latter.

I am well aware that the ſubject of religious diſtinction is a dangerous and delicate topic, eſpecially when applied to a country ſuch as Ireland; the ſituation of which is different in this reſpect from that of every other. Where the eſtabliſhed religion of the State is the ſame as the general religion of the Empire, and where the property of the Country is in the hands of a comparatively ſmall number of perſons profeſſing that eſtabliſhed religion, while the religion of a great majority

majority of the people is different, it is not eafy to fay, on general principles, what fyftem of Church Eftablifhments in fuch a Country would be free from difficulty and inconvenience. By many I know it will be contended, that the religion profeffed by a majority of the people, would at leaft be entitled to an equality of Privileges. I have heard fuch an argument urged in this Houfe; but thofe who apply it without qualification to the cafe of Ireland, forget furely the principles on which Englifh Intereft and Englifh Connection has been eftablifhed in that Country, and on which its prefent Legiflature is formed. No man can fay, that, in the prefent ftate of things, and while Ireland remains a feparate kingdom, full conceffions could be made to the Catholics, without endangering the State, and fhaking the Conftitution of Ireland to its centre.

On the other hand, without anticipating the difcuffion, or the propriety of agitating the queftion, or faying how foon or how late it may be fit to difcufs it; two propofitions are indifputable: Firft, When the conduct of the Catholics fhall be fuch as to make it fafe for the Government to admit

admit them to the participation of the privileges granted to those of the Established Religion, and when the temper of the times shall be favourable to such a measure. When these events take place, it is obvious that such a question may be agitated in an United, Imperial Parliament, with much greater safety, than it could be in a separate Legislature. In the second place, I think it certain that, even for whatever period it may be thought necessary, after the Union, to withhold from the Catholics the enjoyment of those advantages, many of the objections which at present arise out of their situation would be removed, if the Protestant Legislature were no longer separate and local, but general and Imperial; and the Catholics themselves would at once feel a mitigation of the most goading and irritating of their present causes of complaint.

How far, in addition to this great and leading consideration, it may also be wise and practicable to accompany the measure by some mode of relieving the lower orders from the pressure of Tithes, which in many instances operate at present as a great practical evil, or to make—under

proper

proper Regulations, and without breaking in on the security of the present Protestant Establishment an effectual and adequate provision for the Catholic Clergy, it is not now necessary to discuss. It is sufficient to say, that these and all other subordinate points connected with the same subject, are more likely to be permanently and satisfactorily settled by an United Legislature, than by any local arrangements. On these grounds I contend, that with a view to providing an effectual remedy for the distractions which have unhappily prevailed in Ireland, with a view of removing those causes which have endangered, and still endanger its security, the measure which I am now proposing promises to be more effectual than any other which can be devised, and on these grounds alone, if there existed no other, I should feel it my duty to submit it to the House

But, Sir, though what I have thus stated relates most immediately to the great object of healing the dissentions, and providing for the internal tranquillity of Ireland; there are also other objects which, though comparatively with this of inferior importance, are yet in themselves

selves highly material, and in a secondary view, well worthy of attention.

I have heard it asked, when I pressed the measure, what are the positive advantages that Ireland is to derive from it? To this very question I presume the considerations which I have already urged afford a sufficient answer. But, in fact, the question itself is to be considered in another view; and it will be found to bear some resemblance to a question which has been repeatedly put, by some of the Gentlemen opposite to me, during the last six years. What are the advantages which Great Britain has gained by the present war with France?

To this, the brilliant successes of the British army by sea and land, our unexampled naval victories over all our enemies, the solid acquisition of valuable territory, the general increase of our power, the progressive extension of our commerce, and a series of events more glorious than any that ever adorned the page of our history, afford at once an ample and a satisfactory answer. But there is another general answer which we have

have uniformly given, and which would alone be sufficient: it is, that we did not enter into this war for any purpose of ambition; our object was not to acquire, but to preserve; and in this sense, what we have gained by the war is, in one word, ALL that we should have lost without it: it is, the preservation of our Constitution, our Independence, our Honour, our Existence as a Nation.

In the same manner I might answer the question with respect to Ireland, I might enumerate the general advantages which Ireland would derive from the effects of the Arrangement to which I have already referred, the Protection which she will secure to herself in the hour of danger. The most effectual means of increasing her Commerce and improving her Agriculture, the command of English Capital, the infusion of English Manners and English Industry, necessarily tending to ameliorate her Condition, to accelerate the progress of internal civilization, and to terminate those feuds and dissentions which now distract the Country, and which she does not possess, within herself, the power either to controul or to extinguish. She would see the avenue to Honours, to distinctions, and exalted Situations in the general seat of Empire, opened to all those whose abilities and talents enable them to indulge an honourable and laudable ambition.

But, independent of all these advantages, I might also answer, that the question is not what Ireland is to gain, but what she is to preserve: not merely how she may best improve her situation, but how she is to avert a pressing and immediate danger. In this view, what she gains is the preservation of all those blessings arising from the British Constitution, and which are inseparable from her Connexion with Great Britain. Those Blessings of which it has long been the aim of France, in conjunction with domestic traitors, to deprive her, and on their ruins to establish (with all its attendant miseries and horrors) a Jacobin Republic, founded on French Influence, and existing only in subserviency to France.

Such, Sir, would be the answer, if we direct our attention only to the question of general advantage. And here I should be inclined to stop; but since it has also been more particularly asked, what

what are the advantages which she is to gain, in point of Commerce and Manufactures, I am desirous of applying my answer more immediately and distinctly to that part of the subject: and, as I know that the statement will carry more conviction with it, to those who make the inquiry, if given in the words of the Right Honourable Gentleman, to whom, and to whose opinions, I have had more than one occasion to advert in the course of this night, I will read you an extract from his recorded sentiments on the subject, in the year 1785, on this same memorable occasion of the Commercial Propositions. Speaking of a solid and unalterable Compact between the two Countries, speaking expressly of the peculiar importance of insuring the continuance of those Commercial benefits, which she at that time held only at the discretion of this country, he says—
" The exportation of Irish Products to England,
" amounts to Two Millions and a Half annually;
" and the exportation of British Products, to Ire-
" land, amounts to but One Million."

He then proceeds to reason upon the advantage which Ireland would derive, under such circumstances.

cumstances, from guarding against mutual prohibitions; and he accompanies the statement, which I have just read, with this observation—

"If, indeed, the Adjustment were to take away the Benefit from Ireland it would be a good cause for rejecting it; but, as it for ever confirms all the Advantages we derived from our Linen Trade, and binds England from making any law that can be injurious to it, surely Gentlemen who regard that trade, and *whose fortunes and rents depend on its prosperity, will not entertain a moment's doubt about embracing the offer.*"

Such was the reasoning of the Irish CHANCELLOR of the EXCHEQUER; which I consider to have been perfectly just. With reference to his late opinions, I do not think I can more forcibly reply, to a person who signs his name to Propositions which declare that the ruin of the Linen Trade of Ireland is likely to be the consequence of an Union, than by opposing to him his own opinion. I shall be able to strengthen the former opinion of that Gentleman, by stating, that the progress that

that has been made in commercial advantages to Ireland, since 1785, has been such as to render his argument still more applicable. What is the nature of that Commerce, explained by the same person, in so concise and forcible a manner, that I am happy to use his own statement? He does not confine himself to the gross amount, but gives the articles in detail:—

"Britain," he says, "imports annually from
"us Two Million Five Hundred Thousand
"Pounds of our Products, all, or very nearly all,
"duty free, and covenants never to lay a duty on
"them. We import about a Million of her's,
"and raise a Revenue on almost every article of
"it, and reserve the power of continuing that
"Revenue. She exports to us Salt for our
"Fisheries and Provisions; Hops, which we
"cannot grow; Coals which we cannot raise;
"Tin, which we have not; and Bark, which we
"cannot get elsewhere: and all these without re-
"serving any duty."

I will not tire the patience of the House, by reading farther extracts; but the Right Honourable

able Gentleman's whole Speech, in like manner, points out the advantages of the Commercial Propofitions (at that time under confideration) as a ground-work of a Compact between the two Countries, in 1785, on Commercial fubjects.— But how ftands the cafe now? The trade is at this time infinitely more advantageous to Ireland. It will be proved, from the documents which I hold in my hand, as far as relates to the mere interchange of manufactures, that the manufactures, exported to Ireland from Great Britain, in 1797, very little exceeded a Million fterling (the articles of produce amount to nearly the fame fum) while Great Britain, on the other hand, imported from Ireland to the amount of near Three Millions in the manufactured articles of Linen and Linen Yarn, and between Two and Three Millions in Provifions and Cattle, befides Corn and other articles of produce.

In addition to thefe Articles, there are other circumftances of advantage to Ireland. Articles which are effential to her trade and to her fubfiftence, or ferve as raw materials for her manufactures, are fent from hence free of duty. It is ex-
prefsly

prefsly stated on the same authority, that all that we take back from Ireland was liable to a Duty in that country on their exports; so that in some instances we gave them a preference over ourselves.

The increasing produce of the chief article of their manufacture, and four-fifths of her whole export trade, are to be ascribed, not to that *Independent Legislature*, but to the liberality of the British Parliament. It is by the free admission of Linens for our market, and the Bounties granted by the British Parliament on its re-export, that the Linen-Trade has been brought to the height at which we now see it. To the Parliament of this Country, then, it is now owing, that a Market has been opened for her Linen to the amount of three millions. By the Bounty we give to Ireland, we afford her a double market for that article, and (what is still more striking and important) we have prevented a competition against her, arising from the superior cheapness of the Linen-Manufactures of the Continent, by subjecting their importation to a Duty of thirty per cent. Nothing would more clearly shew what would be the danger to Ireland from the Competition in all its principal branches of the Linen-Trade, than the simple fact, that we even now import foreign Linens, under this heavy duty, to an amount equal to a seventh part of all that Ireland is able to send us, with the preference that has been stated. By this arrangement alone, we must therefore be considered, either as foregoing between seven and eight hundred thousand pounds per annum in revenue, which we should collect if we chose to levy the same duty on all Linens, Irish as well as Foreign, or on the other hand, as sacrificing perhaps at least a million sterling in the price paid for those articles, by the subjects of this Country, which might be saved, if we allowed the importation of all Linen, Foreign as well as Irish, equally free from Duty.

The present measure is, however, in its effects calculated not merely for a confirmation of the advantages on which the person to whom I have alluded has insisted. It is obvious that a fuller and more perfect connexion of the two countries, from whatever cause it may arise, must produce a greater facility and freedom of commercial intercourse,

tercourſe, and ultimately tend to the advantage of both. The benefits to be derived to either country from ſuch an arrangement muſt indeed, in a great meaſure, be gradual; but they are not on that account the leſs certain, and they cannot be ſtated in more forcible language than in that uſed in the ſpeech to which I have referred.—

"Gentlemen undervalue the reduction of Bri-
"tiſh Duties on our Manufactures. I agree with
"them it may not operate ſoon, but we are to
"look forward to a final ſettlement, and it is im-
"poſſible but that in time, with as good climate,
"equal natural powers, cheaper food, and fewer
"taxes, we muſt be able to ſell to them. When
"commercial jealouſy ſhall be baniſhed by final
"ſettlement, and trade take its natural and ſteady
"courſe, the Kingdoms will ceaſe to look to
"rivalſhip, each will make that fabrick which it
"can do cheapeſt, and buy from the other what
"it cannot make ſo advantageouſly. Labour
"will be then truly employed to profit, not di-
"verted by Bounties, Jealouſies, or Legiſlative
"Interference, from its natural and beneficial
"courſe. This ſyſtem will attain its real object,
"con-

" confolidating the ftrength of the remaining
" parts of the Empire, by encouraging the com-
" munications of their market among themfelves
" with preference to every part againft all
" ftrangers!"

I am at leaft, therefore, fecure from the defign of appearing to deliver any partial or chimerical opinion of my own, when I thus ftate, on the authority of a perfon the beft informed, and who then judged difpaffionately, both the infinite importance to Ireland of fecuring permanently the great commercial advantages which fhe now holds at the difcretion of Great Britain, and the additional benefit which fhe would derive from any fettlement which opened to her gradually a ftill more free and compleat commercial intercourfe with this country. And while I ftate thus ftrongly the commercial advantages to the fifter kingdom, I have no alarm left I fhould excite any fentiment of jealoufy here. I know that the inhabitants of Great Britain wifh well to the profperity of Ireland;—that, if the Kingdoms are really and folidly united, they feel that to increafe the commercial wealth of one Country is not to diminifh

that

that of the other, but to increafe the ftrength and power of both. But to juftify that fentiment, we muft be fatisfied that the wealth we are pouring into the lap of Ireland is not every day liable to be fnatched from us, and thrown into the fcale of the enemy. If therefore Ireland is to continue, as I truft it will for ever, an effential part of the integral ftrength of the Britifh Empire; if her ftrength is to be permanently ours, and our ftrength to be hers, neither I, nor any Englifh minifter, can ever be deterred by the fear of creating jealoufy in the hearts of Englifh men, from ftating the advantages of a clofer Connexion, or from giving any affiftance to the Commercial Profperity of that Kingdom.

If ever indeed I fhould have the misfortune to witnefs the melancholy moment when fuch principles muft be abandoned, when all hope of feeing Ireland permanently and fecurely conneded with this country fhall be at an end, I fhall at leaft have the confolation of knowing, that it will not be the want of temper or forbearance, of conciliation, of kindnefs, or of full explanation on our part,
which

which will have produced an event so fatal to Ireland, and so dangerous to Great Britain. If ever the over-bearing power of prejudice and passion shall produce that fatal consequence, it will too late be perceived and acknowledged, that all the great commercial advantages which Ireland at present enjoys, and which are continually increasing, are to be ascribed to the liberal conduct, the fostering care, of the British Empire, extended to the sister kingdom as to a part of ourselves, and not (as has been fallaciously and vainly pretended) to any thing which has been done or can be done by the independent power of her own separate Legislature.

I have thus, Sir, endeavoured to state to you the reasons, why I think this measure adviseable; why I wish it to be proposed to the Parliament of Ireland, with temper and fairness; and why it appears to me, entitled at least to a calm and dispassionate discussion in that Kingdom. I am aware, however, that objections have been urged against the measure, some of which are undoubtedly plausible, and have been but too successful in their influence on the Irish Parliament. Of these objections I shall now proceed, as concisely as possible, to take some notice.

The first is, what I heard alluded to by the Honourable Gentleman opposite to me, when his Majesty's Message was brought down; namely That the Parliament of Ireland is incompetent to entertain and discuss the question, or rather, to act upon the measure proposed, without having previously obtained the consent of the people of Ireland, their Constituents. But, Sir, I am led to suppose from what the Honourable Gentleman afterwards stated, that he made this objection, rather by way of deprecating the discussion of the question, than as entertaining the smallest doubt upon it himself. —If, however, the Honourable Gentleman, or any other Gentleman on the other side of the House, should seriously entertain a doubt on the subject, I shall be ready to discuss it with him distinctly, either this night or at any future opportunity. For the present I will assume, that no man can deny the competency of the Parliament of Ireland (representing as it does, in the

language

language of our Constitution, "*lawfully, fully, and freely, all the estates of the people of the realm"*) to make Laws to bind that people, unless he is disposed to distinguish that Parliament from the Parliament of Great Britain; and, while he maintains the independence of the Irish Legislature, yet denies to it the lawful and essential powers of Parliament. No man who maintains the Parliament of Ireland to be co-equal with our own, can deny its competency on this question, unless he means to go the length of denying, at the same moment, the whole of the authority of the Parliament of Great Britain—to shake every principle of legislation—and to maintain, that all the acts passed, and every thing done by Parliament, or sanctioned by its authority, however sacred, however beneficial, is neither more nor less than an act of usurpation. He must not only deny the validity of the union between Scotland and England, but he must deny the authority of every one of the proceedings of the limited Legislature since the Union; nay, Sir, he must go still farther, and deny the authority under which we now sit and deliberate here, as a House of Parliament. Of course, he must deny the validity of the adjustment of 1782, and call

in

in question every measure which he has himself been the most forward to have enforced. This point, Sir, is of so much importance, that I think I ought not to suffer the opportunity to pass, without illustrating more fully what I mean. If this principle of the incompetency of Parliament to the decision of the Measure be admitted, or if it be contended, that Parliament has no legitimate authority to discuss and decide upon it, you will be driven to the necessity of recognizing a principle, the most dangerous that ever was adopted in any civilized State. I mean the principle, that Parliament cannot adopt any measure new in its nature, and of great importance, without appealing to the constituent and delegating authority for directions. If that doctrine be true, look to what an extent it will carry you. If such an argument could be set up and maintained, you acted without any legitimate authority when you created the representation of the Principality of Wales, or of either of the Counties Palatine of England. Every Law that Parliament ever made, without that appeal, either as to its own Frame and Constitution, as to the qualification of the electors or the elected, as to

I the

the great and fundamental point of the fucceffion to the Crown, was made without due authority.

If we turn to Ireland itfelf, what do Gentlemen think of the power of that Parliament, which, without any frefh delegation from its Proteftant conftituents, affociates to itfelf all the Catholic electors, and thus deftroys a fundamental diftinction on which it was formed? God forbid, that I fhould object to or blame any of thefe Meafures! I am only ftating the extent to which the principle (that Parliament has no authority to decide upon the prefent Meafure) will lead; and, if it be admitted in one cafe, it muft be admitted in all. Will any man fay, that (although a Proteftant Parliament in Ireland, chofen exclufively by Proteftant Conftituents, has by its own inherent power, and without confulting thofe couftituents, admitted and comprehended the Catholics who were till then, in fact, a feparate community) that Parliament cannot affociate itfelf with another Proteftant community, reprefented by a Proteftant Parliament, having one intereft with itfelf, and fimilar in its Laws, its Conftitution, and its

Eftablifhed

Established Religion? What must be said by those who have at any time been friends to any plan of Parliamentary Reform, and particularly such as have been most recently brought forward, either in Great Britain or Ireland? Whatever may have been thought of the propriety of the Measure, I never heard any doubt of the competency of Parliament to consider and discuss it. Yet I defy any man to maintain the principle of those plans, without contending that, as a Member of Parliament, he possesses a right to concur in disfranchising those who sent him to Parliament, and to select others, by whom he was not elected, in their stead. I am sure that no sufficient distinction, in point of principle, can be successfully maintained for a single moment; nor should I deem it necessary to dwell on this point, in the manner I do, were I not convinced that it is connected in part with all those false and dangerous notions on the subject of Government which have lately become too prevalent in the world. It may, in fact, be traced to that gross perversion of the principles of all political society, which rests on the supposition that there exists continually in every Government a Sovereignty *in abeyance* (as it were) on the part of the People, ready to be called forth on every occasion, or rather, on every pretence, when it may suit the purposes of the party or faction who are the advocates of this doctrine to suppose an occasion for its exertion. It is in these false principles that are contained the seeds of all the misery, desolation, and ruin, which in the present day have spread themselves over so large a proportion of the habitable Globe.

These principles, Sir, are, at length, so well known and understood in their practical effects, that they can no longer hope for one enlightened or intelligent advocate, when they appear in their true colours. Yet, with all the horror we all feel, in common with the rest of the World, at the effect of them, with all the confirmed and increasing love and veneration which we feel towards the Constitution of our Country, founded as it is, both in Theory and Experience, on principles directly the reverse; yet, there are too many among us, who, while they abhor and reject such opinions, when presented to them in their naked deformity, suffer them in a more disguised shape

to

to be gradually infused into their minds, and insensibly to influence and bias their sentiments and arguments on the greatest and most important discussions. This concealed poison is now more to be dreaded than any open attempt to support such principles by argument or to enforce them by arms. No society, whatever be its particular form, can long subsist, if this principle is once admitted. In every Government, there must reside somewhere a supreme, absolute, and unlimited authority. This is equally true of every lawful Monarchy—of every Aristocracy—of every pure Democracy (if indeed such a form of Government ever has existed, or ever can exist)—and of those mixed Constitutions formed and compounded from the others, which we are justly inclined to prefer to any of them. In all these Governments, indeed alike, that power may by possibility be abused, but whether the abuse is such as to justify and call for the interference of the people collectively, or, more properly speaking, of any portion of it, must always be an extreme case and a question of the greatest and most perilous responsibility, not in Law only, but in Conscience and in Duty, to all those who either act upon it
themselves,

themselves, or persuade others to do so. But no provision for such a case ever has been or can be made before-hand; it forms no chapter in any known code of laws, it can find no place in any system of human jurisprudence. But, above all, if such a principle can make no part of any established Constitution, not even of those where the Government is so framed as to be most liable to the abuse of its powers, it will be preposterous indeed to suppose that it can be admitted in one where those powers are so distributed and balanced as to furnish the best security against the probability of such an abuse. Shall that principle be sanctioned as a necessary part of the best Government, which cannot be admitted to exist even as a check upon the worst! Pregnant as it is with danger and confusion, shall it be received and established in proportion as every reason which can ever make it necessary to recur to it is not likely to exist? Yet, Sir, I know not how it is, that, in proportion as we are less likely to have occasion for so desperate a remedy, in proportion as a Government is so framed as to provide within itself the best guard and control on the exercise of every branch of authority, to furnish the means

of

of preventing or correcting every abuse of power, and to secure, by its own natural operation, a due attention to the interest and feelings of every part of the community, in that very proportion persons have been found perverse enough to imagine, that such a Constitution admits and recognizes, as a part of it, that which is inconsistent with the nature of any Government, and above all, inapplicable to our own.

I have said more, Sir, upon this subject than I should have thought necessary, if I had not felt that this false and dangerous mockery of the *Sovereignty of the People* is in truth one of the chief elements of Jacobinism, one of the favourite impostures to mislead the understanding, and to flatter and inflame the passions of the mass of mankind, who have not the opportunity of examining and exposing it, and that as such on every occasion, and in every shape in which it appears, it ought to be combated and resisted by every friend to civil order, and to the peace and happiness of mankind.

Sir, the next and not the least prevalent objection, is one which is contained in words which are an appeal to a natural and laudable, but what
I must

I muſt call an erroneous and miſtaken ſenſe of national pride. It is an appeal to the generous and noble paſſions of a nation eaſily inflamed under any ſuppoſed attack upon its honour, I mean the attempt to repreſent the queſtion of a Union by compact between the Parliaments of the two Kingdoms as a queſtion involving the Independance of Ireland.—It has been ſaid, that no compenſation could be made to any country for the ſurrender of its National Independance. Sir, on this, as well as on every part of the queſtion, I am deſirous Gentlemen ſhould come cloſely to the point, that they ſhould ſift it to the bottom, and aſcertain upon what grounds and principles their opinion really reſts. Do they mean to maintain that in any humiliating, in any degrading ſenſe of the word which can be acted upon practically as a rule, and which can lead to any uſeful concluſion, that at any time when the Government of any two ſeparate Countries unite in forming one more extenſive empire, that the individuals who compoſe either of the former narrow ſocieties are afterwards leſs members of an independant country, or to any valuable and uſeful purpoſe leſs poſſeſſed of political freedom or

civil

civil happiness than they were before. It must be obvious to every Gentleman who will look at the subject, in tracing the history of all the countries, the most proud of their present existing independance, of all the nations in Europe, there is not one that could exist in the state in which it now stands, if that principle had been acted upon by our forefathers; and Europe must have remained to this hour in a state of ignorance and barbarism, from the perpetual warfare of independent and petty states. In the instance of our own Country, it would be a superfluous waste of time to enumerate the steps by which all its parts were formed into one Kingdom; but will any man in general assert, that in all the different Unions which have formed the principal states of Europe, their inhabitants have become less free, that they have had less of which to be proud, less scope for their own exertions, than they had in their former situation. If this doctrine is to be generally maintained, what becomes of the situation at this hour of any one county of England, or of any one county of Ireland, now united under the independant Parliament of that Kingdom? If it be pushed to its full extent, it is obviously incompatible with all civil society. As the former principle of the fovereignty of the people ſtrikes at the foundation of all governments, ſo this is equally hoſtile to all political confederacy, and mankind muſt be driven back to what is called the ſtate of nature.

But while I combat this general and abſtract principle, which would operate as an objection to every union between ſeparate ſtates, on the ground of the ſacrifice of independance, do I mean to contend that there is in no caſe juſt ground for ſuch a ſtatement? Far from it: it may become, on many occaſions, the firſt duty of a free and generous people. If there exiſts a country which contains within itſelf the means of military protection, the naval force neceſſary for its defence, which furniſhes objects of induſtry ſufficient for the ſubſiſtence of its inhabitants, and pecuniary reſources adequate to maintaining, with dignity, the rank which it has attained among the nations of the world; if, above all, it enjoys the bleſſings of internal content and tranquillity, and poſſeſſes a diſtinct conſtitution of its own, the defects of which, if any, it is within itſelf capable of correcting, and if that conſtitution be equal, if not ſuperior, to that of any other in the world, or (which is nearly the ſame thing)

thing) if those who live under it believe it to be so, and fondly cherish that opinion, I can indeed well understand that such a country must be jealous of any measure, which, even by its own consent, under the authority of its own lawful government, is to associate it as a part of a larger and more extensive empire.

But, Sir, if, on the other hand, it should happen that there be a country which, against the greatest of all dangers that threaten its peace and security, has not adequate means of protecting itself without the aid of another nation; if that other be a neighbouring and kindred nation, speaking the same language, whose laws, whose customs, and habits are the same in principle, but carried to a greater degree of perfection, with a more extensive commerce, and more abundant means of acquiring and diffusing national wealth; the stability of whose government—the excellence of whose constitution—is more than ever the admiration and envy of Europe, and of which the very Country of which we are speaking can only boast an inadequate and imperfect resemblance;—under such circumstances, I would ask, what conduct would be prescribed by every

rational

rational principle of dignity, of honour, or of interest? I would afk, whether this is not a faithful defcription of the circumftances which ought to difpofe Ireland to a Union? Whether Great Britain is not precifely the nation with which, on thefe principles, a Country, fituated as Ireland is, would defire to unite? Does a Union, under fuch circumftances, by free confent, and on juft and equal terms, deferve to be branded as a propofal for fubjecting Ireland to a foreign yoke?— Is it not rather the free and voluntary affociation of two great Countries, which join, for their common benefit, in one Empire, where each will retain its proportional weight and importance, under the fecurity of equal laws, reciprocal affection, and infeparable interefts, and which want nothing but that indiffoluble Connection to render both invincible.

> Non ego nec Teucris Italos parere jubebo
> Nec nova regna peto; paribus fe legibus ambæ
> Invictæ gentes æterna in fœdera mittant.

Sir, I have nearly ftated all that is neceffary for me to trouble the Houfe with; there are, however, one or two other objections which I wifh not entirely to pafs over: One of them is, a

general

general notion that a Union with Great Britain must neceffarily increafe one of the great evils of Ireland, by producing depopulation in many parts of the Country, and by increafing greatly the number of abfentees. I do not mean to deny that this effect would, to a limited extent, take place during a part of the year; but I think it will not be difficult for me to prove, that this circumftance will be more than counterbalanced by the operation of the fyftem in other refpects.

If it be true that this meafure has an inevitable tendency to admit the introduction of that Britifh Capital which is moft likely to give life to all the operations of Commerce, and to all the improvements of Agriculture; if it be that which above all other confiderations is moft likely to give fecurity, quiet, and internal repofe to Ireland; if it is likely to remove the chief bar to the internal advancement of wealth and of civilization, by a more intimate intercourfe with England; if it is more likely to communicate from hence thofe habits which diftinguifh this Country, and which, by a continued gradation, unite the higheft and the loweft orders of the community without a chafm in any part of the fyftem; if it

is

is not only likely to invite (as I have already said) English Capital to set Commerce in motion, but to offer it the use of new markets, to open fresh resources of wealth and industry; can wealth, can industry, can civilization increase among the whole bulk of the people without its much more than counterbalancing the partial effect of the removal of the few individuals who, for a small part of the year, would follow the seat of Legislation? Will it be supposed that the mere absence of Parliament from Dublin, if it would still remain the centre of Education and of the internal commerce of a country increasing in improvement; if it would still remain the seat of legal discussion, which must always increase with an increase of property and occupation, what ground is there to suppose, with a view even to the interests of those whose partial interests have been most successfully appealed to; what reason is there to suppose that, with a view either to the respectable Body of the Bar, to the Merchant, or Shopkeeper of Dublin (if it were possible to suppose that a transaction of this sort ought to be referred to that single criterion) that they would not find their proportionate share of advantage in the general

advantage

advantage of the State? Let it be remembered also, that if the transfer of the Seat of Legislature may call from Ireland to England the Members of the United Parliament, yet, after the Union, property, influence and confideration in Ireland will lead, as much as in Great Britain, to all the objects of imperial ambition; and there muft, confequently, exist a new incitement to perfons to acquire property in that Country, and to thofe who poffefs it, to refide there and to cultivate the good opinion of thofe with whom they live, and to extend and improve their influence and connections.

But, Sir, I need not dwell longer on argument, however it may fatisfy my own mind, becaufe we can on this queftion refer to experience. I fee every Gentleman anticipates that I allude to Scotland. What has been the refult of the Union there? A Union, give me leave to fay, as much oppofed, and by much the fame arguments, prejudices, and mifconceptions, as are urged, at this moment, creating too the fame alarms, and provoking the fame outrages, as have lately taken place in Dublin. Look at the

metropolis

metropolis of Scotland: the population of Edinburgh has been more than doubled since the Union, and a new city added to the old. But we may be told, that Edinburgh has engrossed all the commerce of that country, and has those advantages which Dublin cannot expect. Yet while Edinburgh, deprived of its Parliament, but retaining, as Dublin would retain, its Courts of Justice; continuing, as Dublin would continue, the resort of those whose circumstances would not permit them to visit a distant metropolis; continuing, as Dublin would continue, the seat of national education, while Edinburgh has baffled all the predictions of that period, what has been the situation of Glasgow? The population of Glasgow, since the Union, has increased in the proportion of between five and six to one: look at its progress in manufactures; look at its general advantages, and tell me what ground there is, judging by experience in aid of theory, for those gloomy apprehensions which have been so industriously excited.

There remains, Sir, another general line of argument, which I have already anticipated, and I hope answered, that the commercial privileges now

now enjoyed by Ireland, and to which it owes so much of its prosperity, would be less secure than at present. I have given an answer to that already, by stating that they are falsely imputed to the independence of the Irish Parliament, for that they are in fact owing to the exercise of the voluntary discretion of the British Parliament, unbound by compact, prompted only by its natural disposition to consider the interests of Ireland the same as its own; and if that has been done while Ireland is only united to us in the imperfect and precarious manner in which it is, while it has a separate Parliament, notwithstanding the commercial jealousies of our own manufactures; if under these circumstances we have done so, if we have done so with no other connection than that which now subsists, and while Ireland has no share in our representation; what fresh ground can there be for apprehension, when she will have her proportionate weight in the Legislature, and will be united with us as closely as Lancashire or Yorkshire, or any other county in Great Britain.

Sir, I have seen it under the same authority to which I am sorry so often to advert, that the

L

Linen

Linen Trade would be injured, and that there will be no security for its retaining its present advantages. I have already stated to you (and with that very authority in my favour) that those advantages are at present precarious, and that their security can only arise from Compact with Great Britain. Such a Compact, this Measure would establish in the most solemn manner; but besides this, Sir, the natural policy of this Country, not merely its experienced liberality, but the identity of Interests after a Union, would offer a security worth a thousand Compacts.

Sir, the only other general topic of objection is (that upon which great pains have been taken to raise an alarm in Ireland) the idea that the main principle of the Measure was to subject Ireland to a load of Debt and an increase of Taxes, and to expose her to the consequences of all our alledged difficulties and supposed necessities.

Sir, I hope the zeal, the spirit, and the liberal and enlarged policy, of this Country, has given ample proof that it is not from a pecuniary motive that we seek an Union. If it is not
desirable

desirable on the grounds I have stated, it cannot be recommended for the mere purpose of Taxation; but to quiet any jealousy on this subject, here again let us look to Scotland: is there any instance where, with 45 Members on her part and 513 on ours, that that part of the United Kingdom has paid more than its proportion to the general burthens?—Is it then, Sir, any ground of apprehension, that we are likely to tax Ireland more heavily when she becomes associated with ourselves?—To tax in its due proportion the whole of the Empire, to the utter exclusion of the idea of the predominence of one part of society over another, is the great characteristic of British Finance, as Equality of Laws is of the British Constitution.

But, Sir, in addition to this, if we come to the details of this proposition, it is in our power to fix, for any number of years which shall be thought fit, the proportion by which the Contribution of Ireland, to the expences of the State, shall be regulated; that these proportions shall not be such as would make a contribution greater than the necessary amount of its own present necessary expences as a separate Kingdom; and, even after that limited period, the proportion of the whole contribution, from time to time, might be made to depend on the comparative produce, in each Kingdom, of such general taxes as might be thought to afford the best criterion of their respective wealth. Or, what I should hope would be found practicable, the system of internal taxation in each county might gradually be so equalized and assimilated, on the leading articles, as to make all rules of specific proportion unnecessary, and to secure, that Ireland shall never be taxed but in proportion as we tax ourselves.

The application of these principles, however, will form matter of future discussion; I mention them only as strongly shewing, from the misrepresentation which has taken place on this part of the subject, how incumbent it is upon the House to receive these propositions, and to adopt, after due deliberation, such resolutions as may record to Ireland the terms upon which we are ready to meet her. And, in the mean time, let us wait, not without impatience, but without dissatisfaction, for that moment, when the effect of reason and
discussion

discussion may reconcile the minds of men, in that Kingdom, to a Measure which I am sure will be found as necessary for their peace and happiness, as it will be conducive to the general security and advantage of the British Empire.

Sir, it remains to be my duty to lay these Relutions before the House, wishing that the more detailed discussion of them may be reserved to a future day.

RESOLUTIONS.

FIRST.

That in order to promote and secure the essential Interests of Great Britain and Ireland, and to consolidate the Strength, Power, and Resources of the British Empire, it will be adviseable to concur in such measures as may best tend to unite the two Kingdoms of Great Britain and Ireland into one Kingdom, in such manner, and on such Terms and Conditions as may be established by Acts of the respective Parliaments of His Majesty's said Kingdoms.

SECOND.

That it appears to this Committee that it would be fit to propose as the first Article to serve as a Basis of the said Union, that the said Kingdoms of Great Britain and Ireland shall, upon a day to be agreed upon, be united into one Kingdom, by the name of the UNITED KINGDOM OF GREAT BRITAIN AND IRELAND.

THIRD.

THIRD.

That for the fame purpofe it appears alfo to this Committee, that it would be fit to propofe that the Succeffion to the Monarchy and the Imperial Crown of the faid United Kingdoms, fhall continue limited and fettled, in the fame manner as the Imperial Crown of the faid Kingdoms of Great Britain and Ireland now ftands limited and fettled, according to the exifting Laws, and to the Terms of the Union between England and Scotland.

FOURTH.

That for the fame purpofe it appears alfo to this Committee, that it would be fit to propofe that the faid United Kingdom be reprefented in one and the fame Parliament, to be ftiled the Parliament of the United Kingdom of Great Britain and Ireland, and that fuch a number of Lords Spiritual and Temporal, and fuch a number of Members of the Houfe of Commons as fhall be hereafter agreed upon by Acts of the refpective Parliaments as aforefaid, fhall fit and vote in the faid Parliament on the part of Ireland, and fhall be fummoned, chofen and returned, in fuch manner as fhall be fixed by an Act of the Parliament of Ireland previous to the faid Union; and that every Member hereafter to fit and vote in the faid Parliament of the United Kingdom fhall, until the faid Parliament fhall otherwife provide, take and fubfcribe the fame Oaths, and make the fame Declarations as are by Law required to be taken, fubfcribed and made by the Members of the Parliaments of Great Britain and Ireland.

FIFTH.

That for the fame purpofe it appears alfo to this Committee, that it would be fit to propofe that the Churches of England and Ireland, and the Doctrine, Worfhip, Difcipline, and Government thereof, fhall be preferved as now by Law Eftablifhed.

SIXTH.

That for the fame purpofe it appears alfo to this Committee, that it would be fit to propofe that His Majefty's Subjects in Ireland fhall at all times hereafter be entitled to the fame privileges, and be on the fame footing in refpect of Trade and Navigation, in all Ports and Places belonging to Great Britain, and in all cafes with refpect to which Treaties fhall be made by His Majefty, his Heirs or Succeffors, with any Foreign Power, as His Majefty's Subjects in Great Britain; that no Duty fhall be impofed on the Import or Export between Great Britain and Ireland of any Articles now Duty free: and that on other Articles there fhall be eftablifhed, for a time to be limited, fuch a moderate rate of equal Duties as fhall, previous to the Union, be agreed upon and approved by the refpective Parliaments, fubject, after the expiration of fuch limited time, to be diminifhed equally with refpect to both Kingdoms, but in no cafe to be encreafed; that all Articles which may at any time hereafter be imported into Great Britain from Foreign Parts, fhall be importable through either Kingdom into the other, fubject to the like Duties and Regulations as if the fame were imported directly from Foreign Parts; that where any Articles, the growth, produce, or manufacture of either Kingdom, are fubject to any internal Duty in one Kingdom, fuch countervailing Duties (over and above any Duties on import to be fixed as aforefaid) fhall be impofed as fhall be neceffary to prevent any inequality in that refpect: and that all other matters of Trade and Commerce other than the foregoing, and than fuch others as may before the Union be fpecially agreed upon for the due encouragement of the Agriculture and Manufactures of the refpective Kingdoms, fhall remain to be regulated from time to time by the United Parliament.

SEVENTH.

That for the like purpose it would be fit to propose, that the charge arising from the payment of the Interest or Sinking Fund for the reduction of the Principal of the Debt incurred in either Kingdom before the Union, shall continue to be separately defrayed by Great Britain and Ireland respectively. That for a number of Years to be limited, the future ordinary expences of the UNITED KINGDOM, in Peace or War, shall be defrayed by Great Britain and Ireland jointly, according to such proportions as shall be established by the respective Parliaments previous to the Union; and that after the expiration of the time to be so limited, the proportion shall not be liable to be varied, except according to such rates and principles as shall be in like manner agreed upon previous to the Union.

EIGHTH.

That for the like purpose it would be fit to propose, that all Laws in force at the time of the Union, and that all the Courts of Civil or Ecclesiastical Jurisdiction within the respective Kingdoms, shall remain as now by Law established within the same, subject only to such alterations or regulations from time to time as circumstances may appear to the Parliament of the UNITED KINGDOM to require.

That the foregoing RESOLUTIONS be laid before His Majesty with an humble ADDRESS, assuring His Majesty that we have proceeded with the utmost attention to the consideration of the important objects recommended to us in His Majesty's Gracious MESSAGE.

That we entertain a firm persuasion that a COMPLETE AND INTIRE UNION between Great Britain and Ireland, founded on equal and liberal principles, on the similarity

of

of Laws, Conſtitution and Government, and on a ſenſe of mutual Intereſts and Affections, by promoting the Security, Wealth and Commerce of the reſpective Kingdoms, and by allaying the diſtractions which have unhappily prevailed in Ireland, muſt afford freſh means of oppoſing at all times an effectual reſiſtance to the deſtructive Projects of our Foreign and Domeſtic Enemies, and muſt tend to confirm and augment the Stability, Power, and Reſources of the Empire.

Impreſſed with theſe conſiderations, we feel it our duty humbly to lay before his Majeſty ſuch Propoſitions as appear to us beſt calculated to form the baſis of ſuch a ſettlement, leaving it to His Majeſty's wiſdom, at ſuch time and in ſuch manner as His Majeſty, in his Parental Solicitude for the happineſs of his People, ſhall judge fit, to communicate theſe Propoſitions to His Parliament of Ireland, with whom we ſhall be at all times ready to concur in all ſuch Meaſures as may be found moſt conducive to the accompliſhment of this great and ſalutary Work. And we truſt that, after full and mature conſideration, ſuch a Settlement may be framed and eſtabliſhed, by the deliberative Conſent of the Parliaments of both Kingdoms, as may be conformable to the Sentiments, Wiſhes, and real Intereſts of His Majeſty's faithful Subjects of Great Britain and Ireland, and may unite them inſeparably in the full enjoyment of the bleſſings of our free and invaluable Conſtitution, in the ſupport of the Honour and Dignity of His Majeſty's Crown, and in the preſervation and advancement of the Welfare and Proſperity of the whole Britiſh Empire,

APPENDIX.

The following Message was presented in the House of Commons by Mr. Fox, Secretary of State, on the 9th of April, 1782.

GEORGE R.

HIS Majesty being concerned to find that discontents and jealousies are prevailing among his loyal Subjects in Ireland, upon matters of great weight and importance, earnestly recommends to this House, to take the same into their most serious consideration, in order to such a Final Adjustment as may give mutual satisfaction to both Kingdoms.

G. R.

1st May

1ſt May, 1782.

Mr. Secretary Fox preſented to the Houſe, by His Majeſty's command,

Copy of the Meſſage to the Houſe of Lords and Commons in Ireland, from His Grace the Lord Lieutenant of Ireland, delivered the 16th April, 1782: And alſo,

Copy of a Reſolution of the Houſe of Lords in Ireland, Mercurii, 17° die Aprilis, 1782: And alſo,

Copy of a Reſolution of the Houſe of Commons in Ireland, Martis, 16° die Aprilis, 1782.

And the Titles of the ſaid Copies were read.

The ſaid Copies are as followeth; *viz*.

Copy of the Meſſage to the Houſes of Lords and Commons in Ireland, from His Grace the Lord Lieutenant, delivered the 16th April, 1782.

PORTLAND,

I have it in command from His Majeſty, to inform this Houſe, that His Majeſty being con-

concerned to find that discontents and jealousies are prevailing among his loyal Subjects of this Country, upon matters of great weight and importance, His Majesty recommends to this House to take the same into their most serious consideration, in order to such a Final Adjustment as may give mutual satisfaction to his Kingdoms of Great Britain and Ireland.

P.

Copy of a Resolution of the House of Lords in Ireland, Mercurii, 17° die Aprilis, 1782.

RESOLVED, By the Lords Spiritual and Temporal in Parliament assembled *Nemine dissentiente*, That an humble Address be presented to His Majesty, to return him our thanks for the most gracious Message sent to this House by his Majesty's command, through the medium of His Grace the Lord Lieutenant, and to assure him of our most unshaken loyalty and attachment to His Majesty's person and government, and of the lively sense we entertain of his paternal care of his people of Ireland, in thus enquiring into the

discontents

discontents and jealousies that subsist amongst them, in order to such Final Adjustment as may give mutual satisfaction to his kingdoms of Great Britain and Ireland.

That, thus encouraged by his Royal Interposition, we shall beg leave, with all duty and affection, to lay before His Majesty the cause of such discontents and jealousies.

To represent to His Majesty, That His Subjects of Ireland are entitled to a free constitution; that the Imperial Crown of Ireland is inseparably annexed to the Crown of Great-Britain, on which Connection the happiness of both nations essentially depends; but that the Kingdom of Ireland is a distinct dominion, having a Parliament of her own, the sole Legislature thereof.

That there is no power whatsoever competent to make laws to bind this nation, except the King, Lords, and Commons, of Ireland; upon which exclusive Right of Legislation we consider the very essence of our liberties to depend, a Right which we claim as the Birth-right of the People of Ireland,

land, and which we are determined, in every situation of life, to assert and maintain.

To represent to His Majesty, That we have seen with concern certain claims, both of legislature and judicature, asserted by the Parliament of Great Britain, in an Act passed in Great Britain in the sixth year of George the First, intituled " An Act for the better securing the Depen-" dency of Ireland upon the Crown of Great " Britain:"

That we conceive the said Act, and the powers thereby claimed, to be the great and principal causes of the discontents and jealousies that subsist in this Kingdom:

To assure His Majesty, That this House considers it as a matter of constitutional right and protection, that all Bills which become Law should receive the approbation of His Majesty, under the Seal of Great Britain; but we consider the practice of suppressing our Bills in the Council of Ireland, or altering them any where, to be a matter which calls for redress:

To

To reprefent to His Majefty, That an Act intituled " An Act for the better Accommodation " of His Majefty's Forces;" being unlimited in duration, but which, from the particular circumftances of the times, paffed into a law, has been the caufe of much jealoufy and difcontent in this Kingdom:

That we have thought it our duty to lay before His Majefty thefe, the principal caufes of the difcontents and jealoufies fubfifting in this Kingdom:

That we have the greateft reliance on His Majefty's wifdom, the moft fanguine expectations from his virtuous choice of a Chief Governor, and the greateft confidence in the wife and conftitutional Council His Majefty has adopted:

That we have, moreover, a high fenfe and veneration for the Britifh Character, and do therefore conceive, that the proceedings of this country, founded as they are in right, and fupported by conftitutional liberty, muft have excited the approbation and efteem of the Britifh nation:

That

That we are the more confirmed in this hope, inasmuch as the people of this Kingdom have never expressed a desire to share the freedom of Great Britain, without at the same time declaring their determination to share her fate, standing or falling with the British nation.

Wm. Watts Gayer } Cler.
Edw. Gayer } Parliament.

Copy of a Resolution of the House of Commons in Ireland, Martis, 16° die Aprilis, 1782.

RESOLVED, That an humble Address be presented to His Majesty, to return His Majesty the thanks of this House for his most gracious message to this House, signified by his Grace the Lord Lieutenant. To assure His Majesty of our unshaken attachment to His Majesty's Person and Government, and of our lively sense of his Paternal Care, in thus taking the lead to administer content to His Majesty's subjects of Ireland; that thus encouraged by his royal interposition, we shall beg leave, with all duty and affection, to lay before His Majesty the causes of our discontents

tents and jealousies: To assure His Majesty, that his subjects of Ireland are a free People; that the Crown of Ireland is an Imperial Crown, inseparably annexed to the Crown of Great Britain, on which Connexion the interests and happiness of both Nations essentially depend; but that the kingdom of Ireland is a distinct Kingdom, with a Parliament of her own, the sole Legislature thereof; that there is no body of men competent to make Laws to bind this nation, except the King, Lords, and Commons of Ireland, nor any other Parliament which hath any authority or power of any sort whatsoever in this country, save only the Parliament of Ireland: To assure His Majesty, that we humbly conceive, that in this Right the very Essence of our Liberties exist; a Right which we, on the part of all the People of Ireland, do claim as their birth-right, and which we cannot yield but with our lives: To assure His Majesty, that we have seen with concern certain Claims advanced by the Parliament of Great Britain, in an act, intituled, An Act for the "better securing the Dependency of Ireland;" an act containing matter entirely irreconcileable to the fundamental Rights of this Nation; that we confider this act, and the claims it advances, to be the great and principle caufe of the difcontents and jealoufies in this Kingdom: To affure His Majefty, that His Majefty's Commons of Ireland do moft fincerely wifh, that all Bills which become Law in Ireland fhould receive the approbation of His Majefty, under the Seal of Great Britain; but that yet we do confider the Practice of fuppreffing our Bills in the Council of Ireland, or altering the fame any where, to be another juft caufe of difcontent and jealoufy: To affure His Majefty, that an Act, intituled, "An Act for the better Accommodation of His Majefty's Forces," being unlimitted in duration, and defective in other inftances (but paffed in that fhape from the particular circumftances of the times) is another juft caufe of difcontent and jealoufy in this Kingdom: That we have fubmitted thefe, the principal caufes of the prefent difcontent and jealoufy in Ireland, and remain in humble expectation of redrefs; that we have the greateft reliance on His Majefty's wifdom, the moft fanguine expectations from his virtuous choice of a Chief Governor, and great confidence in the wife, aufpicious, and conftitutional councils

which

which we see with satisfaction His Majesty has adopted; that we have moreover a high sense and veneration for the British character, and do therefore conceive, that the proceedings of this country, founded as they are in right, and tempered by duty, must have excited the approbation and esteem, instead of wounded the pride, of the British Nation; and we beg leave to assure His Majesty, that we are the more confirmed in this hope, inasmuch as the people of this Kingdom have never expressed a desire to share the freedom of England, without declaring a determination to share her fate likewise, standing and falling with the British nation.

   THO. ELLIS, *Cler. Par. Dom. Com.*

ORDERED, That the said Copies do lie upon the Table, to be perused by the Members of the House.

17th May, 1782.

RESOLVED, That this House will, immediately, resolve itself into a Committee of the whole House,

Houfe, to take into confideration His Majefty's moft gracious Meffage, of the 9th Day of April laft, relative to the State of Ireland.

ORDERED, That the feveral papers which were prefented to the Houfe, by Mr. Secretary Fox, upon the 1ft day of this inftant May, be referred to the faid Committee.

Then the Houfe refolved itfelf into the faid Committee.

Mr. Speaker left the Chair.

Mr. Powys took the Chair of the Committee.

Mr. Speaker refumed the Chair.

Mr. Powys reported from the Committee, That they had come to feveral Refolutions; which they had directed him to report, when the Houfe will pleafe to receive the fame.

ORDERED, That the Report be now received.

Mr.

Mr. Powys accordingly reported, from the said Committee, the Resolutions which the Committee had directed him to report to the House, which he read in his place, and afterwards delivered in at the Clerk's table; where the same were read; and are as follows: *viz.*

RESOLVED, That it is the Opinion of this Committee, That an Act, made in the sixth year of the reign of his late Majesty King George the First, intituled, " An Act for the better " securing the Dependency of the Kingdom of " Ireland upon the Crown of Great Britain," ought to be repealed.

RESOLVED, that it is the Opinion of this Committee, That it is indispensible to the interests and happiness of both Kingdoms, that the Connexion between them should be established, by mutual consent, upon a solid and permanent Basis.

The said Resolutions, being severally read a second time, were, upon the Question severally put thereupon, agreed to by the House, *Nemini Contradicenti.*

ORDERED,

ORDERED, That leave be given to bring in a Bill for repealing an Act made in the sixth year of the reign of his late Majesty, King George the First, intituled "An Act for the better securing the Dependency of the Kingdom of Ireland upon the Crown of Great Britain;" and that Mr. Secretary Fox, Mr. Thomas Pitt, Mr. Powys, and Lord John Cavendish, do prepare and bring in the same.

RESOLVED, That an humble Address be presented to His Majesty, That His Majesty will be graciously pleased to take such measures as His Majesty in His Royal Wisdom shall think most conducive to the establishing, by mutual consent, the Connexion between this Kingdom and the Kingdom of Ireland upon a solid and permanent basis.

ORDERED, That the said Address be presented to His Majesty, by such Members of this House as are of His Majesty's most honourable Privy Council.

22d *May*,

22d *May*, 1782.

Mr. Secretary Fox reported to the House, That His Majesty had been attended with the Address of this House, of Friday last, which His Majesty had been pleased to receive very graciously; and that His Majesty had commanded him to acquaint this House, that he will immediately take such measures as may be most likely to conduce to the establishment of a Connexion between this Kingdom and the Kingdom of Ireland upon a solid and permanent basis.

HOUSE OF COMMONS OF IRELAND.

August 12, 1785.*

―――― *The Chancellor of the Exchequer* [Mr. FOSTER] said, he could not sit silent when he heard a measure in which he was proud to have had a considerable part, represented by so many gentlemen as injurious to the independence of the Irish legislature, and a barter of the constitution for commerce. He should think himself, indeed, unworthy of a seat in that House, or of the name of Irishman, if he could consent to barter an atom of the constitution of his country for all the commerce in the world; but he was so fully satisfied the present measure did not violate it, in the smallest degree, that he could not repress his surprise at its being supposed to do so. When gentlemen said, that it violated the constitution, they forgot that they had recorded a similar violation of it in every session, since the freedom of

* " That leave be given to bring in a Bill, for effectuat-
" ing the intercourse and commerce between Great Britain
" and Ireland, on permanent and equitable principles, for the
" mutual benefit of both Kingdoms."

their

their legislation had been established. His Right Hon. Friend (the Attorney General) had quoted the resolution of that House in 1779. He would now read a part of the statute of 1781, made in consequence of that resolution:

" And whereas such part of the trade between this kingdom and the British Colonies in America, the West Indies, and British Settlements on the coast of Africa, as was not enjoyed by this kingdom, previous to the last session of Parliament, can be enjoyed and have continuance so long, and in such case only, as goods to be imported from the said Colonies, Plantations, or Settlements into this kingdom, or to be exported from this kingdom to the said Colonies, Plantations, or Settlements shall be liable to equal duties and drawbacks, and be subject to the same securities, regulations and restrictions as the like goods are liable and subject to, upon being imported from the said Colonies, Plantations, or Settlements into Great Britain, or exported from thence to such Colonies, Plantations, or Settlements respectively; be it enacted by the authority aforesaid, for the advancement of the said trade, that duties, drawbacks, prohibitions, &c. be granted, &c."

This statute passed at a time when the spirit of the nation was as high as ever it had been, and her jealousy of the constitution as great, and has been repeated every session since. Now, Sir, the condition as to regulating trade is as express in this statute as in the present bill. [*Mr. Grattan interrupting,*

interrupting, defired to know what trade?]—*The Chancellor proceeded*, the Plantation trade—the very trade now in agitation; and if accepting trade on conditions would deftroy the conftitution, our conftitution has been long fince deftroyed, even in the very year of its emancipation. But the Right Hon. Gentleman acknowledges the condition which he inveighs againft as being moft dangerous now, to be fimilar to that one which he then and ever fince has deemed fo innocent. He only dwells on its extending to foreign trade, that is, to foreign colonies, as if the greater or lefs extent could change its conftitutional or unconftitutional nature; but will Gentlemen confider the matter, ftripped of all oratory and declamation? Great Britain has colonies, fhe offers full communication of her trade to Ireland, on conditions of Ireland trading on the fame terms as fhe does herfelf; one of thofe terms is equal duties and regulations, which the gentlemen admit to be fair and harmlefs, for we have complied with it in part thefe two feffions; another of the terms is the giving a like protection, as Great Britain gives to their produce againft the produce of foreign colonies. This too is fair, but it deftroys

our

our constitution—what pitiful reasoning! It does not destroy us to receive a monopoly of their consumption; but to give them a monopoly of our consumption, annihilates our independence. No man of common sense can hesitate that it is fair we should receive the trade on the same terms as Britain. The Colonies are hers—she has a right to annex those terms. The trade with them is a gift from her, and the gift is conditional; she offers to take us into partnership in their trade; she, an old established country, raised by commerce alone to an height above any other European power, invites us to partake of the means that raised her to wealth and greatness, to a full and equal share in that trade which cost her millions to obtain and will cost her millions to preserve; and this she does without desiring any thing towards that cost, or for their maintenance, or any return, save a small share of what may arise from our profits in that new partnership. But when gentlemen argue on bad ground, even their own arguments often make against them, and an Hon. Gentleman (Mr. Flood) at the same time that he exerts all his eloquence to persuade us that the confining

ourselves

ourselves to the British Colonies or accepting the trade on such conditions is injurious to the constitution, not only admits but contends, that we have done it already, and that we have done it on the solemn faith of compact. Hear his reasoning; he says, that the transaction of 1780 was a compact, and not a gift, and he says it was a compact, because we gave a consideration; three considerations, each of more value than the gift; we gave monopoly for monopoly, that is, in other words, we agree to prohibit the goods of other colonies, the very thing that is now held up as a surrender of legislature, and the fact is, we did, and still do prohibit, by heavy duties, the same as Britain pays, all foreign colony produce. In theory, therefore, we have agreed to whas he now says cannot be agreed to without ruin, and in practice we have actually done the very thing without injury, if not with benefit to the trade. His other considerations are curious; we gave revenue, and that is, we received liberty to import an article, sugars, that would bear a considerable revenue, which we must have otherwise imposed, elsewhere, and thus he strangely construes the accepting the means of a

revenue

revenue into giving one. His third consideration is still more wonderful; we gave loyalty. Good Heavens; in an Irish House of Commons does he say that we gave our duty to our Prince as a partner for a grant of trade?

Mr. *Flood* interrupted to say, that he had quoted the Resolution of the British Parliament, when he stated, that the loyalty of Ireland was deemed a consideration.

——— *The Chancellor of the Exchequer* resumed. To such wretched shifts are gentlemen driven, who attempt to support what is not supportable, and would vainly endeavour to persuade you that this measure trenches on the independence of our Legislature; you need not adopt any laws that Great Britain may pass for the regulation of commerce; if you do not approve them, you may reject them whenever you think proper; you do but reject the benefit of the condition, and return to the situation in which you now are; but the same Member has proved most strongly the necessity of introducing the Bill, for when such abilities as his can totally mis-

conceive

conceive its tendency, it ought to be introduced, in order to be fully underſtood. He has obſerved largely on each Propoſition, and nothing was ever ſo miſtated, miſrepreſented and miſunderſtood, as every part of them has been by him. It would be abſurd to follow him through all his errors, many of them the moſt ignorant child would be aſhamed to advance; but I will point out a few, not perhaps ſo obvious without examination.

Let me firſt take notice of his having alluded to me, and ſaid, that I voted againſt a declaration of Rights. I deny it; I declared my opinion of the independence of our Legiſlature, from this very ſeat, early in the debate on that day; but did *he* vote for it? *He did not*, and I repeat the Hon. Gentleman did not vote for it, but lamented that the ſubject had been brought in that day.

——I ſhall leave this ſubject as a leſſon to the Hon. Gentleman, never for the future to charge facts that are unfounded. I ſhall now proceed to the Hon. Gentleman's obſervations.

He says " mark the cunning with which the
" resolutions are drawn, to the injury of Ire-
" land; there is no new prohibition to be allow-
" ed on the import from one country to ano-
" ther." This is certainly a great evil, especi-
ally if we consider that the Exportation of Irish
products to England amounts to TWO MILLIONS
and an HALF annually—and the Exportation of
British products to Ireland amount but to ONE
MILLION, so it is injurious to a country which
may by prohibition lose two millions and an
half, to stipulate against prohibitions, and the
country that sends more than she takes, is not
wise in guarding against mutual prohibition.

Another discovery the Hon. Gentleman has
made is that countervailing duties are unfair—why?
Because the Brewery of Ireland will thereby be
effectually protected. The Hon. Gentleman complains of the Report of the English Privy Council, who say that to put Ireland and England on
a footing of exact reciprocity as to linen, Ireland ought to give a bounty on the Exportation
of English Linens, because England gives a
bounty

bounty on the exportation of Irish Linens. Can any thing be more just? Yet England makes no such demand, but is ready by this adjustment to give additional security to our Linen trade for ever. If indeed the adjustment were to take away the benefit from Ireland, it would be a good cause for rejecting it; but as it for ever confirms all the advantages we derive from our Linen trade, and binds England from making any law that can be injurious to it; surely Gentlemen who regard that trade, and whose fortunes and rent depend on its prosperity, will not entertain a moment's doubt about embracing the offer.

Another of his curious objections is, that as we have not a navy of our own, and if we assist the navy of the empire, England will turn that navy to her own ambitious purposes. To what ambitious purposes? To the protection of that commerce, and of those colonies which are now to become ours.—In the moment that she gives up her monopoly of colonies, she is accused of ambitious purpose, for her separate aggrandizement.

The Hon. Gentleman complains, that the Bill now before the English Parliament makes it necessary thay every proper and authentic document to prevent smuggling should be sent by the revenue officers of this country with any foreign or plantation goods sent from hence to England, but that the same precaution is not taken with regard to the same kind of goods sent from England to Ireland. This is the strongest argument for waiting the introduction of the Irish Bill; it speaks the consciousness of the English Parliament, that they could not prescribe to our revenue officers what documents should be satisfactory to them on receiving goods from England, but that the Irish Parliament alone in their own Bill, could determine that matter. It shews the Hon. Gentleman to be totally ignorant of what either is or ought to be the substance of the Bill.

The Hon. Gentleman talks of bounties, and says, by abolishing bounties, we shall no longer be able to bring corn to this city; our inland corn bounties, he says, are to be turned into Protecting Duties for England. A strange conception! But why has he fixed on corn and flour?

If

If he had read the Refolution on which he is arguing, he would have feen that corn and flour are every where exempted.

Another argument of the Hon. Gentleman is, that the declaring that neither country hereafter can lay any new prohibition on native productions, implies cunningly that it may on foreign. What an argument! when the very firft principles of the fyftem is, that a mutual interchange of foreign commodities is for ever to take place between the two kingdoms, and one even of the Twenty Propofitions declares it in precife terms— But, the Hon. Gentleman talks of prohibitions on exports, &c. Would the Hon. Gentleman wifh to leave it in the power of either nation to prohibit their native commodities from being exported to the other? would he wifh to leave it in the power of England to prohibit the exportation of coals, falt, iron, bark, hops, and many other articles, or to raife a revenue on thefe articles when exported hither.

The Hon. Gentleman talks particularly of wool. I admit, if you balance wool againft wool, that

his

his argument is right; but the juft way is to balance the whole of the exports;—England engages never to prohibit the export of articles which are neceffary almoft to our exiftence, and we engage not to prohibit the export of articles which bring us in 500,000l. a year. We are to engage not to prohibit the export of Woollen and Linen Yarn, which we have exported for a whole century, and without keeping a market for the redundancy of which by export, we could *not* enfure plenty for own manufactures.

The Gentleman too totally miftakes the cafe of patents and copy-rights. Britifh patents and copy-rights are protected in Britain by prohibition againft import. The Refolutions fay to us, "protect your's in like manner;" a meafure never yet adopted here, which muft promote genius, printing, and invention in Ireland.

I am afhamed, Sir, of taking up fo much of your time on a fubject which might be fo eafily underftood by the loweft capacity; I fhall therefore quit the Hon. Gentleman and come to the queftion of conftitution, which I do not at all

think

think involved in this subject. If Great Britain grants us a full partnership in all her trade, in all her colonies, if she admits us to a full participation in the benefits of her Navigation laws, by which she has raised herself to the greatest commercial power in the world; if she does not call upon us to contribute to the expence of the partnership, but merely to receive our share of the profits, and says, we may continue in that partnership only so long as we chuse, can any man say, the conditions of it amount to a surrender of our legislature? surely not, it is idle speculation. Let us then look at the subject, free from all imaginary dread for the constitution.

Britain imports annually from us 2,500,000l. of our products; all, or very nearly all, duty free, and covenants never to lay a duty on them. We import about a 1,000,000l. of hers, and raise a revenue on almost every article of it, and reserve the power of continuing that revenue. She exports to us salt for our fisheries and provisions; hops which we cannot grow; coals which we cannot raise; tin which we have not; and bark which we cannot get elsewhere; and all these without

receiving

reserving any duty; or a power to impose any on them; though her own subjects pay 2, 3, or 4s. a chaldron for her own coals, sent coastways, and in London 7s. We on the contrary charge a duty for our own use here on almost every article we send to her. So much for exports; now as to bounties, she almost ruined our manufacture of sail-cloth, by bounties on export of her own to Ireland. In 1750, or thereabouts, when her bounty commenced, we exported more than we imported, and in 1784, we exported none, and imported 180,000 yards; she now withdraws that bounty. And let me digress here a little on sail-cloth, which although gentlemen affect to despise when mentioned, will, I trust, be an immediate source of wealth by this adjustment. For 1. This bounty is to be removed. 2. The export of sail-cloth to the Indies is to be allowed, and Great Britain exported there, in 1782, about 200,000 ells. 3. There is a British law, obliging every British and colony ship to have its first suits of British sail-cloth. Irish now is to be deemed British. 4. There is a preference of 2d. an ell given by British law to British sail cloth, over foreign, for the British navy. Irish is now to have the

same

fame preference. 5. The surplus of the hereditary revenue is to be applied in the first place to the purchase of Irish sail-cloth. All these give a glorious prospect for that valuable manufacture—But to return, were a man to look for the country most advantageous to settle manufacture in, what would be his choice? One where labour and provisions are cheap, that is Ireland; and what he would next look for?—why to have a rich, extended and steady market near him, which England, stretched along-side affords, and to establish that market for this country is one great object of this system. Gentlemen undervalue the reduction of British duties on our manufactures; I agree with them it may not operate soon, but we are to look forward in a final settlement, and it is impossible but that in time, with as good climate, equal natural powers, cheaper food, and fewer taxes, we must be able to sell to them. When commercial jealousy shall be banished by final settlement, and trade take its natural and steady course, the kingdoms will cease to look to rivalship, each will make that fabric which it can do cheapest, and buy from the other what it cannot make so advantageously. Labour will be then truly employed to profit, not diverted by duties, bounties, jealousies or legislative interference from its natural and beneficial course, this system will attain its real object, consolidating the strength of the remaining parts of the empire, by encouraging the communications of their market among themselves, with preference to every part against all strangers.

I need not mention the Navigation Act, the proper benefits of which we have so long looked for; I will only observe, that Great Britain could never agree to receive the British Colonies' goods from us, unless we prohibited the goods of foreign Colonies as she does, which is a powerful argument for that part of the system against the constitutional phrensy that threatens it. Let us also observe, that now, for the first time, Great Britain offers us a right for ever in all present and future Colonies, without any reservation of power, to call on us either to procure, support, or preserve them; *she* maintains them, *we* share all the profits; and not only their goods, but all goods of Irish produce, are to pass through Britain duty free. Can foreign

reign nations, after this is settled, make distinction between British and Irish goods? Our manufactures will be united as our interests, and we shall laugh at Portugal folly.

I could run out for hours into the many benefits of this system but I have tired the House too long; let me only implore you not to reject this measure, for ill-founded, visionary objections, or to sacrifice realities to shadows. If this infatuated country gives up the present offer, she may look for it again in vain; things cannot remain as they are; commercial jealousy is roused, it will increase with two independent legislatures, if they don't mutually declare the principles whereby their powers shall be separately employed, in directing the common concerns of trade; and without an united interest of commerce, in a commercial empire, political union will receive many shocks, and separation of interest must threaten separation of connexion, which every honest Irishman must shudder ever to look at as a possible event.

I will

I will only add, that if this measure be refused, Ireland will receive more solid injury than from any other evil that ever befel her; it is in vain for Gentlemen to think we can go on as we have done for some years—or to expect to cope with England in a destructive war of bounties—our situation must every day become more difficult, and it is impossible to foresee all the ruinous consequences that may ensue. — — —

August 15th, 1785,

Right Hon. *Chancellor of the Exchequer* [Mr. FOSTER] I rise to state the misconception of the Right Hon. Gentleman, and if any thing can shew the necessity of curing the people of their infatuation, by publishing and explaining the Bill to them, it surely is this, that a Gentleman to whom they look up, and justly look, as one whose wisdom and virtue will guard their rights, is so very much mistaken.

The Right Hon. Gentleman in his argument has never once adverted to the Bill on your table,

but

but draws all his conclusions from arguments raised by his own imagination, on the British Resolutions. He dwells now only on foreign Colony trade and Navigation laws; the accepting a full participation of the British Colony trade, upon terms of equal laws, he gives up as not altering our constitution, and he even agrees in the innocence of our declaring it as a principle of the treaty. In this he has shewn his wisdom, for it is already declared in the law of Ireland. The objection then stands as to a foreign Colony trade, and what says the Bill, it declares it to be a condition of the treaty, to protect that trade, in the same manner as Britain does, against the interference of foreign Colony goods. It enacts nothing, and there is the mighty evil which we have introduced, that is to give Britain the regulation of all our foreign trade with Portugal, with Spain, with all the world. If the Gentleman so egregiously mistakes the purport of what he has not read, I trust the good sense of the nation will see his mistakes and judge for themselves; but the objections to an agreement of rating only the goods from foreign Colonies, so far only as by protecting our Colonies against them, is not so wonderful from him as his objection to the Bill's affecting Navigation and British seamen in general; from him I say, for in the year 1782 the Right Hon. Gentleman introduced in conjunction with the late Chief Baron Burgh, and the present Chief Baron Yelverton, a Bill, adopting in the gross all such clauses and provisions of the laws theretofore passed in England, as conveyed equal benefits and imposed equal restrictions in commerce, in the most extended sense, to the subjects of both countries, and also putting the seamen of Ireland on the footing of British seamen. [*The Chancellor here read the words.*] The Bill now brought in does not go so far; he went to commerce in general, and adopted laws without reference to them, or even reciting their title. What does this Bill do? it declares with him the principle; it does no more. This Bill declares for a *similarity of laws*, *manners*, and *customs*, in toto. Our Bill declares for a similarity of Navigation Laws, on our accepting the benefit of the British, not for the first time offered to us. It is idle to believe, even his authority can have weight in such unfounded objections: nay, *our* Bill reaches *his*,

to

to adopt its principles, and he fays our is mifchievous; his was the glory of the nation and the joint labour of the greateft friends of liberty.

The Right Hon. Gentleman fays, " we might have foreign trade, without entering into the meafure, and that England, as to foreign trade, gives us no right which we already have not." As to Colony Trade, he fays, " fhe gives us what we had before, on the former conditions, that we give her Colony product a preference in our market, and therefore, he fays, cannot we remain as we now are."

With refpect to the Colony Trade, I anfwer, we hold it by the gift of Britain, and fhe may repeal her act, and reaffume her monopoly. As to Foreign Trade, I have fhewn it is no way affected, except by the preference to be given to Britifh Colony goods, againft thofe of Foreign Colonies; but why does the Gentleman allude to Portugal? it is the ftrongeft meafure againft him. Portugal has prefumed to diftinguifh between the goods of Great Britain and the goods of Ireland

—fhe

—she will not receive the latter. But if this settlement is entered into, all our goods she can have may go duty free through Britain. The distinction between British and Irish manufacture is lost as to Foreign Nations, our goods, are made one, physically as well as politically, in respect to foreign, and our Union cemented by the freedom of intercourse.

The honourable gentleman seems, with others, to undervalue the British markets for our linens, and that if Britain shall discourage her import, they will find vent elsewhere, I will not pay him so fulsome a compliment as to say he understands commerce, his genius soars perhaps above such reading; but if he did understand it, I would ask him, where would he expect a market to favour the linens of Ireland? Where will he find a market under Heaven for that manufacture, which now brings two millions annually into the kingdom? Will Portugal take them? Will Spain take them? Will France take them? No; we know they will not. Will Russia, Germany, or Holland take them? They are your powerful rivals, and able to undersel you. Where then will

will you find a market, if England shuts her ports? Will you go to the West Indies?—you cannot go to the English Colonies—they will be like Britain—there you can have no admittance. The French, Spanish, and Portuguese have shut their ports long since—your only market then is in the *bankrupt* States of North America, that have not money to pay their just debts, and many provinces of which, if they had the money, have not perhaps the honesty to do it.

This bankrupt country is to give you the market Britain affords: No, no; cherish the market you have, you will never get so good, she ever exports with bounty for you. And here let me observe the benefits of exporting, duty free, all our fabrics through her ports, which this settlement secures. You first found the way for your linens to foreign places through her ports, by her capitals and extent of dealing;—do not refuse the like for your other fabrics—the prosperity of the linen should teach you.

The gentleman says England is as dependant on Ireland as Ireland is on England for her products—he inſtances the cotton yarn and other yarn of Ireland. What, call cotton yarn a fabric of Ireland, and an export to Britain!—It is a miſtake of his expreſſion, he cannot be ſo ignorant of our manufactures. Let us look into the wants Britain ſupplies—I will take coals firſt.

Do you think it an object of no conſequence to receive coals from England, for ever, duty free while, the duties on coals in England, brought from one of her own ports to another is very high. I remember when I propoſed a ſhilling a ton on the importation of coals into Dublin only, in order to raiſe a fund for extending and beautifying the city, it met with great oppoſition; I was abuſed in all the news papers; yet now England may raiſe four times that ſum upon the export of her coals, which will fall upon the conſumer, and raiſe a revenue for her advantage; nay were ſhe even to raiſe the revenue on them to you that ſhe does on her own coaſt carriage, what would become of you? You

have

have not Irish coal; if the present bounty, of 2s. a ton to Dublin, added to 1s. 8d. duty on British, which operates as 3s. 8d. in favour of Irish coal, what will you do; because no carriage can be so cheap to you as that across the channel. Rock salt is the next;—Where will you get it? (some one said from Spain) Rock salt from Spain! The gentleman should inform himself a little better.

As to the tanning trade, where will you get bark? From no place in the world but England. We know that it would not bear the freight from any other, and if England was to prohibit the export of it, that trade must be at an end; and we must not forget, that the British manufacturers of leather have already complained, that by getting bark from Wales, we are enabled to work on as good terms as England.

Let him look to hops; will this country grow them? On the other hand, what wants do we supply for England? wool and linen yarn, to our own great advantage; but it is in vain to proceed; the House must see that we are talking of a subject not yet undeastood; when known, and Ireland

land unprejudiced and in her calm reaſon, will never reject the many bleſſings it holds out to her trade;—it gives wealth and ſecurity which I truſt will never be refuſed from a wild imagination of Utopian Republics, Commonwealths, Monarchies —God knows what.

I will ſtand or fall with the Bill, that not a line in it touches your Conſtitution; it is now left to the deciſion of the country, it is not abandoned, God forbid it ſhould; and I truſt I ſhall ſee the nation aſk it at our hands, that we may be able then to obtain it ſhall be my prayers—the Miniſter cannot promiſe—he has done his duty—and it will be my pride at a future day, when its real value ſhall be known, that I bore a leading ſhare in the tranſaction—that I laboured to procure for Ireland ſolid and ſubſtantial benefits, which even two years ago no man had an idea of even looking to.

www.ingramcontent.com/pod-product-compliance
Lightning Source LLC
Chambersburg PA
CBHW030903170426
43193CB00009BA/722